BANK ON YOURSELF

Unlocking Wealth Through Infinite Banking

Joshua & Candice Harris

Introduction
Rethinking Wealth Management

What if everything you've been taught about money, saving, and investing is wrong? For decades, we've been conditioned to believe that the best way to build wealth is to follow the traditional rules: deposit your earnings into a bank, invest in stocks or mutual funds, and rely on loans from financial institutions to fund your big-ticket expenses. But what if there's a better way? What if you could break free from the cycle of dependence on banks and lenders, grow your wealth predictably, and take full control of your financial future?

Welcome to the world of infinite banking.

The infinite banking concept is more than just a financial strategy; it's a mindset shift—a new way of thinking about and managing money. It challenges conventional wisdom and puts you in the driver's seat, allowing you to become your own banker. Imagine having a financial system where you control the flow of money, leverage your assets to fund your goals, and build a legacy of wealth for generations. It sounds revolutionary, and it is. But it's also entirely achievable.

The Problem with the Traditional System

To understand why infinite banking is so powerful, it's important to examine the flaws in the traditional financial system. Most of us entrust our money to banks, assuming it's the safest and smartest choice. We save diligently, hoping to earn a modest return through interest or investments. Meanwhile, when we need money—for a car, a home, or a business—we turn to banks or credit card companies for loans, paying them back with interest over time.

Here's the problem: banks and financial institutions are designed to profit from you, not empower you. They take your deposits, lend them out at higher interest rates, and pocket the difference. Meanwhile, you're left with minimal returns on your savings and a lifetime of payments on borrowed money. Even when you invest, you're at the mercy of market volatility, unpredictable returns, and often hidden fees.

This system creates a cycle of dependency. You're constantly giving up control of your money and losing out on its full earning potential. Worse yet, every dollar you pay in interest or fees to someone else is a dollar you can't use to grow your own wealth. Over time, the opportunity cost of this system can be staggering.

But what if you could break free from this cycle? What if you could recapture the interest you're currently paying to banks, earn guaranteed growth on your money, and eliminate the stress of market fluctuations? That's exactly what infinite banking allows you to do.

A New Way to Think About Money

The infinite banking concept was pioneered by Nelson Nash, a visionary who realized that the principles of banking could be applied on a personal level. At its core, infinite banking revolves around using a specially designed whole life insurance policy as a financial tool. While most people think of life insurance as a way to protect their family after death, infinite banking transforms it into a dynamic system for building and leveraging wealth.

Here's how it works: when you fund a whole life insurance policy, part of your premiums goes toward building cash value—a savings component that grows over time. This cash value earns guaranteed interest, often supplemented by dividends, and grows tax-free. Unlike a traditional bank account, you can borrow against your cash value at any time, for any purpose, without credit checks or rigid repayment schedules. Meanwhile, your money continues to grow as though you never borrowed it, thanks to the power of uninterrupted compounding interest.

In essence, you're creating your own private banking system—one where you set the terms, keep the profits, and use your money to fund your goals.

The Promise of Infinite Banking

Infinite banking isn't just a financial strategy; it's a pathway to freedom. By taking control of your money, you can eliminate debt, fund major life expenses, and build a secure financial future. But the benefits don't stop there. Infinite banking also offers:

- **Predictable Growth:** Unlike volatile investments, your money grows steadily and predictably within a whole life insurance policy.

- **Tax Advantages:** With proper structuring, your cash value grows tax-deferred, and loans can be accessed tax-free.

- **Flexibility:** Use your policy for anything—from buying a car to starting a business—without asking for permission.

- **Legacy Building:** Pass on wealth to your loved ones while teaching them the principles of financial independence.

This book will guide you step by step through the process of understanding, setting up, and using your own infinite banking system. You'll learn the foundational principles, discover how to design a policy tailored to your needs, and see real-world examples of infinite banking in action. Along the way, we'll address common questions, debunk myths, and equip you with the tools to take full control of your financial destiny.

Why This Book?

The infinite banking concept is often misunderstood or dismissed because it challenges conventional norms. It's not a get-rich-quick scheme or a magic bullet—it's a disciplined, long-term strategy that requires commitment and understanding. That's why this book was written: to provide clarity, guidance, and inspiration for anyone who wants to take control of their financial future.

Whether you're new to infinite banking or looking to deepen your knowledge, this book will serve as your roadmap. By the end, you'll have the confidence and tools to implement this strategy in your own life, creating a financial system that works for you—not the banks.

The journey to financial independence starts here. It's time to bank on yourself.

Part I: The Foundations of Infinite Banking

Chapter 1: What Is Infinite Banking?

Imagine a world where you don't rely on banks, credit cards, or traditional lenders to finance your life. A world where your money works for you at all times, compounding uninterrupted, while you retain full control. This isn't a pipe dream—it's the foundation of the infinite banking concept.

In this chapter, we'll dive into what infinite banking is, how it works, and why it's a transformative approach to managing your finances. By the end, you'll understand the core principles behind infinite banking and why it offers a path to financial independence.

What Is Infinite Banking?

At its core, infinite banking is a strategy that allows you to become your own banker. Instead of depositing money into a traditional bank or borrowing from financial institutions, you create a private banking system using a specially designed whole life insurance policy. This approach enables you to:

- Grow your wealth predictably.

- Recapture interest that would otherwise go to banks or lenders.

- Access your money on your terms.

The concept was popularized by Nelson Nash in his groundbreaking book, *Becoming Your Own Banker*. Nash's vision was simple but revolutionary: individuals could use whole life insurance policies to take control of their financial lives. By understanding how banks operate and applying those principles to your own finances, you could bypass traditional financial systems and build lasting wealth.

How Does It Work?

Infinite banking revolves around three key elements: **saving, leveraging, and compounding.**

1. **Saving:**
   You start by funding a specially designed whole life insurance policy. Unlike typical whole life policies, this one is tailored for maximum cash value growth and liquidity. A portion of your premium builds a cash value—a savings-like account within the policy that grows over time.

2. **Leveraging:**
   Once your cash value builds up, you can borrow against it at any time, for any reason. These loans come with unique advantages:

   - **No credit checks or approval process.**
     Since you're borrowing against your own asset, there's no need to qualify for the loan.

   - **Uninterrupted growth.**
     Even when you borrow, the cash value in your policy continues to grow as if you hadn't touched it.

This is the magic of uninterrupted compounding interest.

- **Flexible repayment terms.**
  You control how and when to repay the loan, with no rigid schedules or penalties.

3. **Compounding:**
   The real power of infinite banking lies in the ability to let your money grow without interruption. Traditional savings accounts and investments often experience interruptions when you withdraw money or face market downturns. With infinite banking, your money stays in the policy, earning guaranteed interest and dividends, even as you use it.

Key Principles of Infinite Banking

To fully grasp infinite banking, it's important to understand its underlying principles:

1. **Control Over Your Money**
   Infinite banking gives you complete control of your finances. Unlike traditional banks,

which dictate how you access and use your money, your policy operates on your terms. You decide when to save, when to borrow, and how to repay.

2. **The Power of Liquidity**
   Liquidity is the ability to access your money when you need it. Infinite banking policies are designed for high liquidity, allowing you to tap into your cash value without penalties or restrictions.

3. **Uninterrupted Compounding Interest**
   The longer your money compounds without interruption, the faster it grows. Infinite banking ensures that your money continues to grow even when you borrow against it.

4. **Recapturing Interest**
   Every time you pay interest to a bank or lender, that money is gone forever. With infinite banking, you recapture that interest because you're essentially borrowing from yourself.

5. **Legacy Building**
   In addition to cash value, your whole life policy provides a death benefit. This ensures that your wealth is passed on to future generations, creating a financial legacy.

Why Whole Life Insurance?

You might be wondering, "Why use a whole life insurance policy for this strategy?" The answer lies in its unique features:

1. **Guaranteed Growth**
   Whole life insurance policies provide guaranteed growth of cash value, regardless of market conditions. This stability makes them an ideal foundation for infinite banking.

2. **Dividends**
   Many policies from mutual insurance companies pay annual dividends, further boosting your cash value growth. While dividends aren't guaranteed, reputable

insurers have a long history of paying them consistently.

3. **Tax Advantages**

    - **Tax-deferred growth:** The cash value in your policy grows tax-free.

    - **Tax-free loans:** Borrowing against your policy does not trigger a taxable event.

    - **Tax-free death benefit:** When you pass away, your beneficiaries receive the death benefit tax-free.

4. **Liquidity and Flexibility**
    Unlike retirement accounts or other long-term savings vehicles, your policy's cash value is always accessible. There are no penalties for early access, and you can use the funds for any purpose.

Who Is Infinite Banking For?

Infinite banking is not a one-size-fits-all solution. It's most effective for individuals who:

- Value financial independence and control.
- Are willing to commit to long-term thinking and disciplined saving.
- Have a desire to build generational wealth.

This strategy is particularly beneficial for:

- Entrepreneurs seeking flexible capital for their businesses.
- Families looking to finance major expenses like college tuition or home purchases.
- Investors who want a stable, predictable foundation for their portfolio.

Is Infinite Banking Right for You?

While infinite banking offers incredible benefits, it requires a mindset shift. It's not a quick fix or a get-rich-quick scheme. Success with infinite banking depends on:

- Understanding the system and its long-term nature.

- Committing to properly funding your policy.

- Being patient as your cash value grows.

If you're ready to take control of your financial future and break free from traditional banking systems, infinite banking could be the key to unlocking your potential.

Conclusion: A New Way to Think About Money

Infinite banking isn't just a financial strategy—it's a philosophy. It's about rethinking how money works and reclaiming control over your financial destiny. By understanding the principles of infinite banking, you're taking the first step toward a life of financial freedom and independence.

In the next chapter, we'll take a closer look at the flaws in the traditional banking system and why so many people remain trapped in a cycle of dependency. By contrasting this with the principles of infinite banking, you'll see why it's time to start banking on yourself.

Chapter 2: The Problem with Conventional Banking

For most of us, the banking system is the default way to manage money. We deposit our paychecks into checking or savings accounts, apply for loans when we need to make large purchases, and rely on credit cards for emergencies or convenience. This system feels intuitive—it's what we've been taught to do. But beneath the surface, conventional banking is designed to benefit the institutions, not you.

In this chapter, we'll examine the mechanics of traditional banking, uncover its flaws, and explain why it keeps so many people trapped in a cycle of financial dependency. By the end, you'll understand why moving away from this system is the first step toward true financial independence.

How Traditional Banks Work

Banks play a critical role in the economy, but their primary purpose is to generate profits for their shareholders—not to build wealth for their customers. Here's how the system works:

1. **Deposits**

    You deposit money into a savings or checking account. In return, the bank promises to keep your money safe and may offer a small amount of interest—often so small that it doesn't keep up with inflation.

2. **Lending**

    The bank uses your deposits to fund loans for other customers. These loans might be for mortgages, car purchases, personal loans, or credit cards. The bank charges borrowers interest, often at significantly higher rates than what they pay you for your deposits.

3. **The Spread**

    The difference between the interest the bank charges borrowers and the interest it pays you is called the "spread." This is how banks make their money. For example, if the bank charges 6% on a mortgage but pays you 0.5% on your savings, it pockets the 5.5% difference.

4. **Fees and Penalties**
   In addition to the spread, banks generate revenue through fees: overdraft charges, ATM fees, account maintenance fees, and penalties for late payments or early withdrawals. These costs can add up quickly for the average customer.

Flaws in the Conventional Banking System

While this system works well for the banks, it often works against you. Let's break down the major flaws:

1. Lost Opportunity Cost

Every dollar you give to the bank—whether through deposits or loan payments—represents a lost opportunity for growth. When your money is tied up in a bank account earning minimal interest or used to pay off debt, it's not working for you. Over time, this lost opportunity compounds, significantly reducing your potential wealth.

2. Dependency on External Lenders

Most people rely on banks and credit card companies to finance major expenses like homes, cars, education, or emergencies. This creates a cycle of dependency where you're perpetually borrowing and repaying, often at high interest rates. The result? A lifetime of payments to financial institutions.

3. Minimal Returns on Savings

Interest rates on savings accounts are often so low that they fail to outpace inflation. For example, if your bank offers a 0.5% interest rate but inflation is 3%, your money is effectively losing value each year. This makes traditional savings accounts a poor vehicle for growing wealth.

4. Loss of Control

When your money is in a bank, you don't have full control over it. Withdrawal limits, transfer delays, and account restrictions can make accessing your money inconvenient. In some cases, like during economic downturns, banks may impose additional restrictions or fees.

5. Exposure to Market Volatility

Many people turn to investments like mutual funds or 401(k) plans to grow their money. While these can offer higher returns than savings accounts, they also expose you to market volatility. A single market crash can wipe out years of gains, leaving you financially vulnerable.

6. Erosion Through Fees and Interest Payments

The average person pays thousands of dollars in fees and interest over their lifetime. For example:

- Credit card interest rates often range from 15% to 25%.

- Mortgage payments can include tens of thousands of dollars in interest over the life of the loan.

- Hidden fees in investment accounts can erode your returns.

All of these costs add up, siphoning wealth away from you and toward financial institutions.

Why This System Persists

If the traditional banking system is so flawed, why does it remain the default option for so many people? The answer lies in a combination of societal norms, lack of financial education, and the convenience that banks offer.

1. **Societal Conditioning**
   From a young age, we're taught to trust banks. Parents open savings accounts for their children, schools teach the basics of banking, and financial institutions market themselves as safe and reliable. This ingrains the belief that banks are the best place to manage money.

2. **Lack of Financial Literacy**
   Most people don't receive formal education about personal finance. As a result, they don't question the inefficiencies of the traditional banking system or explore alternative strategies like infinite banking.

3. **Perceived Convenience**
   Banks offer convenience: direct deposit,

online banking, credit cards, and mobile apps make managing money seem easy. However, this convenience often comes at a high cost in terms of lost opportunity and control.

4. **Marketing and Advertising**
   Banks invest heavily in advertising to maintain their image as essential and trustworthy institutions. This messaging reinforces the idea that traditional banking is the only viable option.

The Cycle of Financial Dependency

The flaws in the conventional banking system create a cycle of financial dependency that's hard to escape:

1. You deposit your money into a bank, earning minimal interest.

2. When you need funds for a major purchase, you borrow from the same bank, paying high interest rates.

3. Your savings grow slowly (if at all), while your debts grow quickly.

4. To fund future expenses, you repeat the cycle, keeping the bank in control of your financial life.

Breaking free from this cycle requires a fundamental shift in how you think about money. Instead of letting banks control your finances, you need to take control and make your money work for you.

Why Infinite Banking Offers a Solution

Infinite banking provides an alternative to the conventional banking system. Instead of relying on external institutions, you create your own private banking system. By doing so, you:

- Retain control over your money.

- Capture the interest that would otherwise go to banks.

- Ensure your money grows uninterrupted, even when you use it.

This approach eliminates the inefficiencies of traditional banking and empowers you to build wealth on your terms.

Conclusion: Time to Rethink Banking

The traditional banking system is not designed to make you wealthy—it's designed to profit from your dependency. If you want to achieve financial independence, you need to stop playing by the bank's rules and start playing by your own.

Infinite banking offers a way out. It's a system that puts you in control, allowing you to recapture lost opportunity costs, avoid debt traps, and grow your wealth predictably. In the next chapter, we'll explore why whole life insurance is the foundation of this system and how it enables you to take the first step toward becoming your own banker.

Chapter 3: Why Whole Life Insurance?

When people hear about infinite banking, their first question often is, *Why whole life insurance?* It's a fair question. Whole life insurance has been misunderstood and even maligned in mainstream financial advice, often dismissed as "too expensive" or unnecessary compared to term life insurance. However, in the context of infinite banking, whole life insurance is not just a life insurance product—it's a financial tool, a cornerstone of a system that empowers you to take control of your money.

In this chapter, we'll explore why whole life insurance is the foundation of infinite banking, how it works, and why it's uniquely suited for this purpose. By the end, you'll understand how a properly designed whole life insurance policy transforms into a private banking system that benefits you for life—and beyond.

The Basics of Whole Life Insurance

Whole life insurance is a type of permanent life insurance that provides:

1. **A Death Benefit:** A guaranteed payout to your beneficiaries when you pass away.

2. **A Cash Value Component:** A savings-like account within the policy that grows over time.

Unlike term life insurance, which provides coverage for a limited period (e.g., 20 or 30 years), whole life insurance remains in effect as long as you pay the premiums. The cash value grows tax-deferred and can be accessed during your lifetime, making it a versatile financial tool.

Why Whole Life Insurance Is Ideal for Infinite Banking

Not all life insurance policies are created equal, and not all are suitable for infinite banking. Whole life insurance, specifically when designed for maximum cash value growth, offers several unique features that make it the ideal vehicle for infinite banking.

1. Guaranteed Growth

Whole life insurance provides guaranteed growth of the cash value, regardless of market conditions. Unlike investments in stocks or mutual funds, which are subject to volatility, the cash value in a whole life policy grows predictably. This stability is critical for creating a reliable banking system.

2. Dividends

When you purchase a whole life policy from a mutual insurance company, you become a part-owner of the company. Mutual insurance companies often pay dividends to policyholders, which can be used to accelerate the growth of your cash value. While dividends aren't guaranteed, many mutual insurers have a long history of paying them consistently, even during economic downturns.

3. Liquidity

One of the most powerful features of whole life insurance is the ability to borrow against the cash value. These policy loans are:

- **Quick and Easy to Access:** No credit checks or approval processes.

- **Flexible in Repayment Terms:** You control when and how to repay the loan, without the risk of penalties.

- **Uninterrupted in Growth:** Even when you borrow against your cash value, the money continues to grow as if it were never touched.

This liquidity gives you financial flexibility and control that traditional savings accounts or investment vehicles cannot match.

4. Tax Advantages

Whole life insurance offers several tax benefits:

- **Tax-Deferred Growth:** The cash value grows without being subject to annual taxes.

- **Tax-Free Loans:** Borrowing against your policy is not considered a taxable event.

- **Tax-Free Death Benefit:** When you pass away, the death benefit is paid to your beneficiaries tax-free, allowing you to leave a legacy.

These advantages make whole life insurance a tax-efficient way to grow and access your wealth.

5. Protection and Legacy

In addition to serving as a financial tool, whole life insurance provides a death benefit that ensures your loved ones are taken care of when you're gone. This dual-purpose feature—wealth-building during your lifetime and wealth transfer after death—sets it apart from other financial instruments.

How Whole Life Insurance Works for Infinite Banking

To understand why whole life insurance is ideal for infinite banking, it's essential to look at how the cash value component operates:

Building Cash Value

When you pay premiums on a whole life insurance policy, a portion of the payment goes toward:

1. **The Death Benefit:** Ensuring your policy provides coverage for your entire life.

2. **Administrative Costs:** Covering the operational costs of the policy.

3. **The Cash Value:** A savings-like account within the policy that grows over time.

In policies designed for infinite banking, the cash value grows faster because they are structured to minimize the cost of the death benefit and maximize the portion allocated to cash value. This requires working with an experienced professional who understands how to structure policies specifically for infinite banking.

Taking Policy Loans

Once your cash value reaches a certain threshold, you can borrow against it. Here's how it works:

1. **You Request a Loan:** Notify the insurance company that you'd like to borrow against your cash value.

2. **Funds Are Disbursed:** The loan is processed quickly, with no credit checks or lengthy paperwork.

3. **Cash Value Continues to Grow:** Even though you've borrowed against it, the cash value remains intact, earning interest and dividends as if the money were never withdrawn.

Repaying the Loan

You have full control over how and when to repay the loan. There are no mandatory repayment schedules or penalties for non-payment. However, it's in your best interest to repay the loan so you can continue using the policy for future needs.

Common Misconceptions About Whole Life Insurance

Whole life insurance often gets a bad rap because of misconceptions and misunderstandings. Let's address some of the most common objections:

1. "It's Too Expensive"

While the premiums for whole life insurance are higher than those for term life, it's important to consider what you're paying for:

- Guaranteed lifetime coverage.
- A growing cash value that you can access during your lifetime.
- The ability to create your own banking system.

When viewed as a financial tool rather than just an insurance product, the cost becomes a worthwhile investment in your financial future.

2. "It Takes Too Long to Build Cash Value"

While it's true that whole life policies take time to build substantial cash value, policies designed for infinite banking are structured differently. By minimizing the cost of the death benefit and maximizing paid-up additions (a way to supercharge cash value growth), these policies build liquidity much faster.

3. "I Can Get Better Returns Elsewhere"

Infinite banking isn't about chasing high returns; it's about creating a stable, predictable financial system that you control. While investments in the stock market may offer higher returns, they come with higher risk and lack the guarantees that whole life insurance provides.

The Role of Mutual Insurance Companies

It's worth emphasizing the importance of choosing the right insurance company. Mutual insurance companies are ideal for infinite banking because they are owned by policyholders, not shareholders. This structure ensures that the company's profits are reinvested in the form of dividends for policyholders, rather than distributed to shareholders.

Key Features of a Properly Designed Policy

Not all whole life insurance policies are suitable for infinite banking. A properly designed policy should:

1. Be issued by a reputable mutual insurance company.

2. Maximize cash value growth through paid-up additions.

3. Minimize the base death benefit to reduce premium costs.

4. Include flexible features that allow you to adjust contributions as needed.

Working with an experienced professional is crucial to ensure your policy is tailored to meet your needs and goals.

Conclusion: The Perfect Tool for Infinite Banking

Whole life insurance is more than just a financial product—it's the foundation of a system that allows you to take control of your money, grow your wealth predictably, and create financial freedom. Its unique combination of guaranteed growth, liquidity, tax advantages, and protection makes it the ideal vehicle for infinite banking.

In the next chapter, we'll explore how to design and fund your own private banking system, ensuring it aligns with your financial goals and sets you on the path to independence. It's time to start thinking of whole life insurance not as an expense, but as an opportunity to build the financial future you deserve.

Part II: Building Your Infinite Banking System

Chapter 4: Designing Your Personal Bank

Creating your own banking system through infinite banking isn't just a financial strategy—it's a mindset shift. To truly take control of your finances, you need to understand how to structure and fund a whole life insurance policy specifically tailored for infinite banking. This chapter will guide you through the process of designing your personal bank, from choosing the right policy to understanding how it functions as a tool for building and leveraging wealth.

By the end of this chapter, you'll have a clear blueprint for setting up your personal banking system and making it work for your financial goals.

Step 1: Choosing the Right Insurance Company

The first and most critical step is selecting the right insurance company. Not all insurance providers are created equal, and the success of your infinite banking system depends on partnering with a company that aligns with your goals.

Key Characteristics of a Suitable Insurance Company

1. **Mutual Insurance Companies**
   Choose a mutual insurance company rather than a stock company. Mutual companies are owned by policyholders and share profits through dividends, which can accelerate your cash value growth.

2. **Strong Financial Ratings**
   Look for companies with high ratings from agencies like A.M. Best, Moody's, or Standard & Poor's. These ratings indicate financial stability and a strong track record of meeting obligations to policyholders.

3. **History of Dividend Payments**
   Select a company with a long history of

consistently paying dividends, even during economic downturns. Dividends aren't guaranteed, but a strong track record is a good indicator of reliability.

4. **Flexibility in Policy Design**
Work with a company that allows customization of policies to maximize cash value growth. Not all insurers offer the flexibility required for infinite banking.

Step 2: Structuring Your Whole Life Policy

A whole life insurance policy for infinite banking must be designed differently than a traditional policy. The goal is to maximize cash value growth while keeping premiums affordable and minimizing costs associated with the death benefit.

Key Components of Policy Design

1. **Base Premium**
The base premium is the primary cost of your policy and covers the death benefit. For infinite banking, this should be minimized to ensure more money goes toward building cash value.

2. **Paid-Up Additions (PUAs)**
   PUAs are additional contributions you can make to your policy to increase the cash value and death benefit. These are critical for maximizing the cash value growth of your policy.

3. **Reduced Death Benefit**
   Infinite banking policies prioritize cash value over a high death benefit. While the death benefit is still important for legacy planning, the primary focus is on creating a liquid, growing asset you can use during your lifetime.

4. **Policy Riders**
   Certain riders can enhance the flexibility and performance of your policy. Key riders include:

   o **Paid-Up Additions Rider:** Allows you to contribute additional premiums to accelerate cash value growth.

- **Waiver of Premium Rider:** Ensures your premiums are covered if you become disabled and can no longer work.

Customizing the Policy for Your Needs

Every person's financial situation is different, so your policy should be tailored to your specific goals. Factors to consider include:

- Your age and health (which affect premiums and insurability).

- How quickly you want to build cash value.

- Your anticipated need for liquidity (e.g., funding a business, paying off debt, or making investments).

- Your long-term financial goals, such as retirement or legacy planning.

Step 3: Funding Your Policy

The funding stage is where your personal banking system begins to take shape. Properly funding your policy is crucial for building cash value quickly and ensuring you have liquidity when you need it.

How Much Should You Fund?

The amount you contribute to your policy depends on your financial capacity and goals. Ideally, you should aim to fund your policy at the ***maximum efficient level***—the highest amount allowed without triggering IRS limits on tax advantages.

Initial Capitalization

Infinite banking requires patience and commitment. In the early years, your premiums go toward both the cost of insurance and the cash value. While the growth may seem slow at first, the benefits compound over time. Think of the first few years as the "capitalization phase" of your bank.

Ongoing Contributions

Consistently funding your policy through base premiums and paid-up additions is essential for building a robust cash value. The more you contribute, the faster your cash value will grow, providing you with greater financial flexibility.

Step 4: Understanding How Your Bank Functions

Once your policy is in place and funded, it's time to understand how it operates as your personal banking system. This involves two key functions: accessing your cash value and repaying policy loans.

Accessing Your Cash Value

The cash value in your policy is the foundation of your banking system. You can access it through policy loans, which offer unique advantages:

1. **No Credit Checks:** Since you're borrowing against your own money, there's no need for credit approval.

2. **Fast Processing:** Loans are typically processed quickly, giving you immediate access to funds.

3. **Uninterrupted Growth:** Even when you borrow against your cash value, the policy continues to grow as though the money were never withdrawn.

Using Policy Loans

Policy loans can be used for any purpose, including:

- Paying off high-interest debt.
- Funding business ventures or investments.
- Covering major life expenses, such as education or home renovations.
- Creating a "bridge loan" during times of financial uncertainty.

Repaying Policy Loans

One of the most flexible aspects of infinite banking is that you set your own repayment terms. While you aren't required to repay the loan immediately, doing so ensures that your cash value remains available for future use. Additionally:

- You can repay loans on your own schedule.
- Payments can be made with interest, allowing you to "recapture" interest payments that would otherwise go to a bank or lender.

Step 5: Tracking and Optimizing Your System

To maximize the benefits of your personal banking system, you need to track and optimize its performance over time. This involves:

1. **Monitoring Cash Value Growth:** Regularly review your policy statements to track the growth of your cash value and dividends.

2. **Strategic Use of Loans:** Plan your loans and repayments to align with your financial goals, ensuring you always have liquidity when needed.

3. **Reinvesting and Recycling Funds:** Use your policy loans to generate income or pay down debt, then reinvest those funds back into your policy to accelerate growth.

The Role of Discipline and Patience

Infinite banking is a long-term strategy that requires discipline and patience. In the early years, the results may seem modest, but over time, the compounding effect of uninterrupted growth creates exponential benefits. Staying committed to funding your policy and managing it wisely is the key to success.

Common Mistakes to Avoid

1. **Underfunding Your Policy:** Failing to contribute enough can limit the growth of your cash value and reduce the effectiveness of your banking system.

2. **Overborrowing:** While policy loans are flexible, borrowing too much without a repayment plan can strain your system.

3. **Choosing the Wrong Insurance Company:** Working with a company that doesn't offer the right policy features can undermine your goals.

4. **Focusing Solely on the Death Benefit:** Remember, the primary goal is to create a living asset you can use during your lifetime.

Conclusion: Building Your Financial Foundation

Designing your personal bank is the first step toward reclaiming control of your finances. By choosing the right insurance company, structuring your policy for maximum cash value, and funding it consistently, you're creating a powerful financial tool that grows predictably and gives you the flexibility to achieve your goals.

In the next chapter, we'll explore how to leverage your banking system to fund major expenses, eliminate debt, and create new income streams, unlocking the full potential of infinite banking.

CHAPTER 5: FUNDING YOUR BANK

Once you've set up your whole life insurance policy as the foundation for your infinite banking system, the next crucial step is funding it effectively. Funding your policy is about more than just paying premiums; it's about building a financial engine that allows you to take control of your money and achieve your financial goals. In this chapter, we'll dive into the strategies for funding your policy, managing cash flow, and maximizing the growth of your cash value.

By the end of this chapter, you'll understand how to capitalize your bank in a way that ensures its long-term sustainability and empowers you to use it as a reliable source of liquidity and wealth-building.

Why Proper Funding Matters

Funding your whole life insurance policy is the most important factor in building a successful infinite banking system. The money you contribute serves two purposes:

1. **Covering the Cost of Insurance:** This ensures your policy stays in force and provides a death benefit for your beneficiaries.

2. **Building Cash Value:** This is the component you'll use as your personal banking system, allowing you to borrow against it, grow it, and leverage it over time.

Underfunding your policy can hinder its growth, while overfunding it without proper structure can lead to tax consequences. Striking the right balance is essential.

Understanding the Two Components of Funding

When you pay premiums on a properly designed whole life insurance policy, your money is allocated in two main ways:

1. Base Premium

The base premium is the foundational cost of your policy. A portion of this payment goes toward the cost of the death benefit and administrative expenses. While it contributes to the cash value, its growth is slower compared to other components of the policy.

2. Paid-Up Additions (PUAs)

PUAs are additional contributions that go directly into building the cash value of your policy. They allow you to "supercharge" your cash value growth while also increasing your death benefit. PUAs are a critical element of infinite banking because they maximize the liquidity of your policy in the early years.

How Much Should You Fund Your Policy?

Determining how much to fund your policy depends on several factors, including your financial situation, goals, and long-term plans. Here are some guidelines to consider:

Start with a Budget

Your first step is to evaluate your current financial situation and determine how much you can comfortably allocate to your policy. A general rule of thumb is to redirect a portion of the money you're already saving or spending on debt repayments.

The MEC Limit

When funding your policy, you must stay below the **Modified Endowment Contract (MEC)** limit. This is an IRS-imposed cap that determines how much money you can put into your policy while maintaining its tax advantages. Exceeding the MEC limit can turn your policy into a taxable investment vehicle.

Aiming for Maximum Efficiency

The most effective infinite banking policies are funded as close to the MEC limit as possible. This ensures you're maximizing the cash value growth while keeping the policy's tax advantages intact.

Incremental Growth

If you can't fully fund your policy from the start, don't worry. Many policies are designed with flexibility, allowing you to increase contributions over time as your financial capacity grows.

Strategies for Funding Your Policy

1. Redirect Existing Cash Flow

One of the simplest ways to fund your policy is to redirect money you're already spending or saving:

- Use funds from existing savings accounts or low-interest investments.

- Reallocate payments you're making toward high-interest debt after paying it off.

2. Start Small and Build Gradually

If you're not in a position to fully fund your policy immediately, start with smaller contributions and increase them over time. Many policies are designed with flexibility to accommodate fluctuating cash flow.

3. Use Windfalls

Lump-sum payments like bonuses, tax refunds, or inheritances can be an excellent way to fund your policy quickly and efficiently. Applying these windfalls to PUAs will accelerate your cash value growth.

4. Business Income

If you're a business owner, you can use business profits to fund your policy. This strategy not only grows your cash value but also provides a source of liquidity for reinvestment in your business.

5. Eliminate Debt

Consider using policy loans to pay off high-interest debt. Once the debt is eliminated, redirect the money you were using for debt payments into funding your policy.

Capitalization Phase: Building Your Bank

In the first few years, your policy will go through what is called the **capitalization phase.** During this time, a significant portion of your premiums will go toward the cost of insurance, which means your cash value growth will be slower. While this phase may seem like a hurdle, it's a necessary step in building a sustainable banking system.

What to Expect During the Capitalization Phase

1. **Limited Liquidity:** Early on, you won't have full access to the cash value of your premiums because part of the funds cover insurance costs.

2. **Gradual Growth:** Cash value growth accelerates over time as more of your contributions go toward PUAs and compounding takes effect.

3. **Dividends Begin to Compound:** As your policy matures, dividends will start to play a larger role in accelerating cash value growth.

The Importance of Patience

Many people get discouraged during the capitalization phase because they don't see immediate results. However, the true power of infinite banking lies in its long-term compounding effect. By staying consistent with your contributions, you'll unlock exponential growth in later years.

Balancing Liquidity and Long-Term Growth

Infinite banking is about creating a balance between immediate access to your cash value and long-term growth. Here's how to strike the right balance:

1. Maintain Flexibility

Life is unpredictable, so it's important to have a policy that allows you to adjust your contributions as needed. For example, during times of financial strain, you can scale back your PUAs while keeping your base premium intact.

2. Avoid Overborrowing

While the liquidity of your cash value is a major benefit, borrowing too much without a repayment plan can hinder your policy's growth. Always borrow with a purpose and a strategy for repayment.

3. Recycle Money Through Your Policy

One of the most effective strategies is to use your cash value for investments or debt elimination, then redirect the returns or savings back into your policy. This creates a self-reinforcing cycle of growth.

Tax Implications and Considerations

Properly funding your policy ensures you retain its tax advantages:

- **Tax-Deferred Growth:** The cash value grows without being taxed annually.

- **Tax-Free Loans:** Borrowing against your policy does not trigger a taxable event.

- **Tax-Free Death Benefit:** Your beneficiaries receive the death benefit tax-free, ensuring your legacy is protected.

To maintain these benefits, it's critical to stay below the MEC limit and work with a knowledgeable advisor to ensure compliance with IRS rules.

Common Pitfalls to Avoid

1. **Underfunding the Policy** Failing to contribute enough to your policy will slow its growth and limit its usefulness as a banking system.

2. **Overfunding Without Proper Structure** Exceeding the MEC limit can result in your

policy losing its tax advantages, turning it into a taxable investment.

3. **Lack of a Long-Term Plan** Infinite banking requires commitment and long-term thinking. Avoid the temptation to abandon your policy during the early capitalization phase.

Conclusion: Laying the Foundation for Success

Funding your policy is the cornerstone of building a successful infinite banking system. By committing to consistent contributions and understanding the balance between short-term liquidity and long-term growth, you're creating a financial tool that empowers you to take control of your money.

In the next chapter, we'll explore how to leverage your banking system to finance major expenses, eliminate debt, and create new opportunities for wealth generation. With your bank funded, the possibilities are limitless.

CHAPTER 6: LEVERAGING YOUR BANK

Now that your whole life insurance policy is set up and funded, it's time to unlock its full potential. The true power of infinite banking lies in leveraging your policy to create opportunities for growth, manage financial challenges, and build wealth. Unlike traditional bank loans or investments, your personal banking system offers unparalleled flexibility, control, and efficiency.

This chapter will walk you through the mechanics of leveraging your bank. You'll learn how to borrow against your policy, when and why to use policy loans, and how to strategically manage repayments to maximize your wealth-building potential.

Understanding Policy Loans

A policy loan allows you to borrow against the cash value of your whole life insurance policy. Here's how it works:

1. **Your Cash Value as Collateral:**
   When you take a loan, you're borrowing against the cash value in your policy, which serves as collateral. The insurance company lends you money, but your cash value remains intact and continues to grow.

2. **Uninterrupted Growth:**
   Unlike withdrawing money from a savings account or selling investments, borrowing against your policy doesn't interrupt the growth of your cash value. This is one of the key benefits of infinite banking.

3. **Loan Terms:**
   - **No Credit Checks:** Loans are granted without a credit check or approval process.

- o **Flexible Repayments:** You set your own repayment terms.

- o **Competitive Interest Rates:** Interest rates on policy loans are generally lower than traditional loans and are paid back into the policy.

4. **Control Over Funds:**
You can use the funds for any purpose—no questions asked. Whether you're paying off debt, investing, or covering unexpected expenses, the choice is yours.

The Benefits of Borrowing Against Your Policy

1. Liquidity Without Sacrifice

Policy loans give you immediate access to cash without liquidating assets or interrupting the growth of your wealth. This allows you to address short-term needs while preserving long-term benefits.

2. Tax-Free Access to Funds

Borrowing against your policy is not considered a taxable event. Unlike withdrawals from retirement accounts or investments, you won't owe taxes on the loan.

3. Recapturing Interest Payments

When you repay your policy loan with interest, that interest goes back into your policy rather than to an external lender. This allows you to "recycle" your money and build wealth more efficiently.

4. Flexibility and Control

Traditional loans come with rigid repayment schedules and penalties for missed payments. With policy loans, you have full control over when and how to repay, giving you financial flexibility.

When to Use Policy Loans

Policy loans can be used for virtually any purpose, but they are particularly effective for strategic financial decisions. Here are some common scenarios:

1. Paying Off High-Interest Debt

Use your policy loan to pay off high-interest debt like credit cards or personal loans. Once the debt is eliminated, redirect the money you were using for payments back into your policy to accelerate cash value growth.

2. Funding Investments

Policy loans can provide capital for investments such as real estate, stocks, or business ventures. The key is to ensure that the returns on your investment exceed the loan interest rate, creating a positive spread.

3. Financing Major Purchases

Rather than taking out an auto loan or home equity loan, use your policy to finance major purchases. You'll avoid traditional lenders and recapture the interest payments.

4. Bridging Cash Flow Gaps

If you're facing a temporary cash flow issue, a policy loan can provide the liquidity you need without relying on external lenders or selling assets.

5. Creating Opportunities

Use your policy as a source of opportunity capital. Whether it's starting a new business, funding education, or seizing a time-sensitive investment opportunity, having access to liquidity gives you the power to act.

Managing Policy Loans

Borrowing against your policy is only part of the equation. Properly managing your loans is critical to ensuring the long-term success of your banking system.

1. Plan Your Repayments

While policy loans don't have mandatory repayment schedules, it's in your best interest to repay them in a timely manner. Doing so replenishes your cash value, making it available for future use.

2. Pay Yourself Back with Interest

When repaying your loan, include interest payments as part of your repayment strategy. This allows you to recapture the cost of borrowing and grow your policy more efficiently.

3. Avoid Overborrowing

While your policy offers significant liquidity, borrowing too much without a clear repayment plan can strain your system. Always borrow within your means and ensure your cash flow supports repayments.

4. Leverage Responsibly

Policy loans are a tool, not a free pass to overspend. Use them strategically to fund opportunities that generate value or eliminate financial burdens.

Case Studies: Policy Loans in Action

Case Study 1: Paying Off Credit Card Debt

- **Scenario:** John has $15,000 in credit card debt with an interest rate of 18%.

- **Solution:** He takes a $15,000 policy loan at a 5% interest rate to pay off the credit card.

- **Outcome:** John eliminates the high-interest debt and redirects his former credit card payment of $500/month into repaying his policy loan. Over time, his policy's cash value grows, and he saves thousands of dollars in interest payments.

Case Study 2: Funding a Real Estate Investment

- **Scenario:** Sarah identifies a real estate deal requiring $50,000 in upfront capital.

- **Solution:** She takes a $50,000 policy loan at 6% interest and invests in the property, earning a 12% annual return.

- **Outcome:** Sarah generates a positive spread of 6% (12% return - 6% loan interest) while her policy's cash value continues to grow uninterrupted.

Case Study 3: Financing a Business

- **Scenario:** Mike wants to start a small business and needs $25,000 for startup costs.

- **Solution:** He uses a policy loan to fund the business, avoiding the need for a traditional business loan.

- **Outcome:** As the business generates profits, Mike repays the loan, effectively using his policy to finance his entrepreneurial dream.

Maximizing the Benefits of Leveraging

1. Compound the Gains

Use the returns from investments or debt savings to reinvest in your policy. This creates a compounding effect that accelerates your wealth-building.

2. Recycle Money Through Your Bank

Treat your policy as a revolving line of credit. Borrow, repay, and reborrow as needed to keep your money working for you at all times.

3. Use a Long-Term Perspective

The benefits of infinite banking compound over time. Stay disciplined and focused on the long-term growth of your system.

Common Pitfalls to Avoid

1. Ignoring Repayments

While repayments are flexible, neglecting them can erode your cash value and reduce the effectiveness of your system.

2. Overleveraging

Borrowing too much can strain your policy and reduce its ability to support future opportunities. Always borrow responsibly.

3. Using Loans for Nonproductive Spending

Avoid using policy loans for unnecessary or nonproductive expenses that don't create value or generate returns.

Conclusion: Unlocking Financial Freedom

Leveraging your policy is the key to unlocking the full potential of infinite banking. By using policy loans strategically, you can eliminate debt, fund investments, and create opportunities that build lasting wealth. The flexibility, control, and uninterrupted growth offered by your personal banking system set it apart from traditional financial strategies.

In the next chapter, we'll explore how to use your banking system to create a perpetual wealth cycle, ensuring that your money works for you across generations. With the power of leverage, your journey to financial independence is just beginning.

Part III: Unlocking Wealth Potential

Chapter 7: Creating a Perpetual Wealth System

Infinite banking isn't just about solving today's financial challenges—it's a strategy for building wealth that lasts a lifetime and beyond. The true power of infinite banking lies in its ability to create a self-sustaining system where money grows, circulates, and compounds uninterrupted. In this chapter, we'll explore how to use your personal banking system to establish a perpetual wealth cycle that not only benefits you but also creates a legacy for future generations.

What Is a Perpetual Wealth System?

A perpetual wealth system is a financial ecosystem you create using your whole life insurance policy as the foundation. It allows you to:

1. Grow your wealth through guaranteed cash value growth and dividends.

2. Recapture and recycle money that would otherwise be lost to interest or fees.

3. Use your money for major expenses, investments, or emergencies without interrupting its growth.

4. Build generational wealth by teaching others how to use and sustain the system.

This approach aligns with the fundamental principles of financial independence: control, liquidity, and uninterrupted growth.

The Core Components of a Perpetual Wealth System

To create a system that sustains itself over time, you need to focus on three key components:

1. Uninterrupted Compounding

The foundation of a perpetual wealth system is uninterrupted compounding. This occurs when your money grows continuously, without being diminished by taxes, withdrawals, or market fluctuations.

- **How It Works in Your Policy:** Even when you borrow against your cash value, the total amount continues to grow as though you never touched it. This is the magic of uninterrupted compounding, which allows your wealth to grow exponentially over time.

2. The Velocity of Money

The velocity of money refers to how quickly and effectively your money circulates within your financial system. In a perpetual wealth system:

- You borrow money from your policy.

- Use it for productive purposes, such as paying off debt, investing, or funding opportunities.

- Repay the policy loan, restoring your cash value and making it available for the next opportunity.

By continually putting your money to work and recapturing it, you create a cycle of growth that accelerates over time.

3. Generational Continuity

A perpetual wealth system isn't just about your financial goals—it's about building a legacy. By structuring your policy and educating future generations, you can pass on both wealth and the knowledge to sustain it.

Steps to Build a Perpetual Wealth System

Step 1: Optimize Your Policy

The first step is ensuring your whole life insurance policy is structured for maximum efficiency:

1. **Maximize Paid-Up Additions (PUAs):** Regularly contribute to PUAs to accelerate cash value growth.

2. **Avoid Overborrowing:** Maintain a healthy cash value balance to ensure uninterrupted growth.

3. **Monitor Policy Performance:** Regularly review your policy to ensure it's performing as expected.

Step 2: Create a Wealth Recycling Process

A key principle of infinite banking is using and reusing your money effectively. Here's how:

1. **Borrow Strategically:** Take loans against your cash value for investments, debt payoff, or major purchases.

2. **Generate Returns:** Ensure the use of the borrowed funds creates value—whether

through investment returns, cost savings, or increased income.

3. **Repay with Interest:** Pay back the loan with interest to replenish your cash value and recapture the opportunity cost.

By continuously cycling money through your policy, you create a financial engine that grows stronger with each use.

Step 3: Integrate Your Policy Into Your Financial Life

A perpetual wealth system isn't just a tool for isolated transactions—it should be integrated into your broader financial strategy:

1. Use your policy as a savings vehicle for short-term goals.

2. Finance major life expenses, such as college tuition or home renovations, through your policy.

3. Build a diversified investment portfolio using policy loans as capital.

Step 4: Establish Multiple Policies

As your financial capacity grows, consider establishing additional whole life insurance policies. Multiple policies:

- Increase your cash value reserves.
- Provide additional borrowing capacity.
- Allow you to create policies for family members, extending the system across generations.

Using Your System for Generational Wealth

A perpetual wealth system isn't just about building wealth for yourself—it's about creating a legacy. Here's how to ensure your system benefits future generations:

1. Educate Your Family

Teach your children and other family members about the principles of infinite banking and how to use the system responsibly. Financial literacy is key to sustaining generational wealth.

2. Establish Policies for Family Members

Consider setting up whole life insurance policies for your children or grandchildren. These policies:

- Build cash value over time, giving them a head start on financial independence.

- Provide a death benefit, ensuring long-term financial security.

3. Use the Death Benefit Wisely

The death benefit from your policy can serve as a financial bridge for your heirs. Use it to:

- Pay off debts.

- Fund additional policies to continue the cycle.

- Invest in opportunities that support long-term family goals.

4. Create a Family Banking System

A family banking system allows multiple generations to leverage the benefits of infinite banking. By pooling resources and sharing knowledge, your family can create a financial ecosystem that sustains itself over time.

The Role of Discipline in a Perpetual Wealth System

A perpetual wealth system requires discipline and a long-term perspective. Key habits to cultivate include:

1. **Consistent Funding:** Regularly contribute to your policy through base premiums and PUAs.

2. **Strategic Borrowing:** Only borrow for productive purposes that align with your financial goals.

3. **Commitment to Repayment:** Treat your policy loans like any other financial obligation to ensure the system remains strong.

The Power of Time: Compounding Over Generations

The true magic of a perpetual wealth system lies in its ability to compound wealth over time. Consider the following:

- In the early years, the system grows steadily as you build cash value and repay loans.

- Over time, the compounding effect accelerates, creating exponential growth.

- When passed to the next generation, the system continues to grow, creating a legacy of financial independence.

By maintaining and expanding the system, you're not just building wealth—you're creating a financial legacy that lasts for generations.

Case Studies: Perpetual Wealth in Action

Case Study 1: Family Banking System

- **Scenario:** The Smith family sets up whole life policies for each family member and pools resources into a family banking system.

- **Outcome:** They use the system to finance college tuition, fund business ventures, and provide down payments for homes. Over two generations, the system grows to support multiple family members without relying on external lenders.

Case Study 2: Multigenerational Wealth

- **Scenario:** John establishes a policy for himself and later sets up policies for his children. Upon his passing, the death benefit funds additional policies for his grandchildren.

- **Outcome:** The family's wealth system grows exponentially, creating financial security and opportunities for generations to come.

Common Pitfalls to Avoid

1. Neglecting the System

Failing to fund, manage, or repay loans can weaken your perpetual wealth system. Treat it as a living, dynamic process that requires regular attention.

2. Overborrowing Without a Plan

Excessive borrowing without a repayment strategy can deplete your cash value and reduce the system's efficiency.

3. Lack of Education

Without proper education, future generations may misuse or fail to sustain the system. Invest time in teaching family members the principles of infinite banking.

Conclusion: A Legacy of Wealth and Independence

A perpetual wealth system isn't just a financial strategy—it's a philosophy of independence, control, and growth. By leveraging your infinite banking system to create a cycle of uninterrupted compounding, velocity, and generational continuity, you're building a financial legacy that empowers you and your family for years to come.

In the next chapter, we'll explore how infinite banking can be applied to real-life scenarios, showcasing the flexibility and power of this strategy in action. With your perpetual wealth system in place, you're well on your way to achieving financial freedom and leaving a lasting impact.

CHAPTER 8: INFINITE BANKING IN ACTION

Understanding the theory of infinite banking is one thing; seeing it applied to real-life situations is another. In this chapter, we'll dive deep into how infinite banking can be used to address common financial needs, overcome challenges, and create opportunities. From paying off debt to funding investments, you'll see how individuals and families have harnessed the power of infinite banking to achieve financial independence and build wealth.

By the end of this chapter, you'll have a clear understanding of the practical applications of infinite banking and how you can implement these strategies in your own life.

Key Applications of Infinite Banking

Infinite banking isn't a one-size-fits-all strategy. Its flexibility allows it to be tailored to meet various financial goals. Here are the most common applications:

1. Debt Elimination

Debt is one of the greatest barriers to financial freedom. Infinite banking provides a way to systematically eliminate high-interest debt while recapturing the interest payments for your benefit.

- **How It Works:**

- Use a policy loan to pay off high-interest debt, such as credit cards or personal loans.
- Redirect the money you were paying toward the debt to repay the policy loan.
- Once the loan is repaid, the cash value is replenished and available for other uses.

- **Example:**
Sarah has $20,000 in credit card debt with an interest rate of 18%. She takes a policy loan at 5% interest to pay off the debt. Over the next two years, she repays the loan using the $600/month she was previously paying to the credit card company. By the end of the repayment period, she has saved thousands in interest and fully restored her cash value.

2. Major Purchases

Infinite banking allows you to finance major purchases—like cars, home improvements, or large equipment—on your terms, without relying on external lenders.

- **How It Works:**
    - Borrow against your cash value to finance the purchase.
    - Repay the loan with interest, treating it as you would a traditional loan.
    - Recapture the interest payments into your policy, rather than paying them to a bank.

- **Example:**
John uses a $30,000 policy loan to purchase a car. He sets up a repayment plan to "pay himself back" $500/month for 60 months at 6% interest. By the end of the loan term, he has recaptured the interest, and his cash value has continued to grow uninterrupted.

3. Funding Investments

Infinite banking can provide the capital needed to invest in opportunities, such as real estate, stocks, or starting a business.

- **How It Works:**
    - Use a policy loan as a source of opportunity capital.
    - Invest in an asset that generates a return greater than the loan interest rate.
    - Repay the policy loan using the returns from the investment.

- **Example:**
Lisa takes a $50,000 policy loan to invest in a rental property that generates $12,000 in annual net income. She repays the loan over five years while maintaining ownership of the property, which continues to generate income and appreciate in value.

4. College Funding

Traditional college savings plans, like 529 accounts, have restrictions on how funds can be used. With infinite banking, you can fund education expenses without limitations.

- **How It Works:**
    - Borrow against your cash value to pay tuition or other educational expenses.
    - Repay the loan on your own terms, potentially using the student's future income to contribute.

- **Example:**
The Smith family uses a $40,000 policy loan to cover their child's college tuition. Once their child graduates and secures a job, they set up a repayment plan where the child contributes to repaying the loan, replenishing the family's cash value.

5. Emergency Fund

Unlike traditional savings accounts, the cash value in your policy serves as a tax-advantaged emergency fund that continues to grow even when accessed.

- **How It Works:**
    - Keep a portion of your cash value available for emergencies.
    - Borrow against it as needed, without penalties or tax implications.
    - Repay the loan on your own timeline to restore liquidity.

- **Example:**
Mark experiences an unexpected medical expense of $10,000. Instead of relying on a credit card, he uses a policy loan to cover the cost. Over the next year, he repays the loan, restoring his cash value and avoiding high-interest debt.

6. Retirement Planning

Infinite banking complements traditional retirement accounts by providing a source of tax-free income in retirement.

- **How It Works:**
    - During your working years, fund your policy and allow the cash value to grow.
    - In retirement, use policy loans as a source of tax-free income.
    - The loans do not need to be repaid during your lifetime, as the death benefit will cover the outstanding balance.

- **Example:**
    Mary uses her policy to supplement her retirement income by taking out $30,000 annually in policy loans. Her cash value continues to grow, and the outstanding loan balance is deducted from the death benefit, leaving her heirs with a substantial legacy.

Real-Life Success Stories

Case Study 1: From Debt to Financial Freedom

- **Background:**
  James and Emily were drowning in $50,000 of credit card and personal loan debt with interest rates averaging 15%.

- **Infinite Banking Solution:**
  They took a $50,000 policy loan at 5% interest to pay off the debt. They redirected their $1,200/month debt payments into repaying the policy loan.

- **Outcome:**
  Within four years, they eliminated their debt and fully restored their cash value. They now use their policy to fund investments and have avoided traditional lenders altogether.

Case Study 2: Building a Real Estate Empire

- **Background:**
  Rebecca, a real estate investor, wanted to

expand her portfolio but didn't want to rely on traditional bank loans.

- **Infinite Banking Solution:**
  She used her policy to finance the down payments for multiple properties. The rental income from the properties covered the loan repayments.

- **Outcome:**
  Over 10 years, Rebecca built a portfolio of 10 properties, generating passive income while her policy's cash value continued to grow.

Case Study 3: Entrepreneurial Success

- **Background:**
  Mike wanted to start his own business but struggled to secure financing from banks.

- **Infinite Banking Solution:**
  He took a $100,000 policy loan to cover startup costs. As his business became profitable, he repaid the loan and later used the policy to fund business expansion.

- **Outcome:**
  Mike's business thrived, and he used his policy to finance growth without relying on external lenders.

The Flexibility of Infinite Banking

Infinite banking is powerful because it adapts to your changing financial needs. Whether you're navigating a financial emergency, pursuing investment opportunities, or planning for retirement, your personal banking system is always there to support you.

Key Benefits in Action

1. **Access Anytime:** Borrow against your cash value without restrictions or penalties.

2. **Tax Advantages:** Enjoy tax-free access to funds and tax-deferred growth.

3. **No Third-Party Control:** You're in complete control of how and when to use your money.

Common Questions About Using Infinite Banking

1. What Happens If I Can't Repay a Policy Loan?

Policy loans don't have mandatory repayment schedules. If you can't repay the loan, the outstanding balance will be deducted from your death benefit. However, repaying loans is in your best interest to maintain liquidity and maximize your policy's potential.

2. Can I Use My Policy for Multiple Purposes?

Yes, your policy is a versatile financial tool. You can use it to address multiple financial goals, often simultaneously, by carefully managing loans and repayments.

3. How Does Borrowing Affect My Policy's Growth?

When you take a policy loan, your cash value continues to grow as if you hadn't borrowed against it. This uninterrupted growth is one of the most significant advantages of infinite banking.

Conclusion: The Power of Application

Infinite banking is more than a financial strategy—it's a lifestyle. By leveraging your policy for debt elimination, investments, major purchases, and other needs, you gain control over your financial future. The real-world applications of infinite banking demonstrate its flexibility, scalability, and potential to transform the way you manage money.

In the next chapter, we'll explore the tax advantages of infinite banking and how to integrate this strategy into a comprehensive plan for financial independence. With your policy in action, you're well on your way to creating a life of abundance and control.

Chapter 9: Tax Advantages and Financial Independence

One of the most compelling aspects of infinite banking is its ability to provide significant tax advantages. By leveraging the unique features of a properly structured whole life insurance policy, you can grow your wealth while legally minimizing your tax burden. In this chapter, we'll delve into the tax benefits of infinite banking, explain how these advantages work, and explore how to use them as part of a broader strategy for achieving financial independence.

The Tax Landscape of Traditional Savings and Investments

Before understanding the tax benefits of infinite banking, it's essential to recognize the tax challenges posed by traditional savings and investment vehicles:

1. **Tax on Earnings:**
   - Interest earned in savings accounts is taxable as ordinary income.
   - Dividends and capital gains from investments are subject to taxes, often eroding your returns.

2. **Tax on Withdrawals:**
   - Withdrawals from retirement accounts like 401(k)s and IRAs are taxed as ordinary income, unless made from a Roth account.
   - Early withdrawals often incur additional penalties.

3. **Estate Taxes:**
   - Traditional assets may be subject to estate taxes, reducing the wealth passed on to your heirs.

These taxes create significant barriers to growing and preserving wealth over time. Infinite banking offers an alternative by leveraging the tax advantages of whole life insurance.

Tax Advantages of Infinite Banking

A properly structured whole life insurance policy provides unique tax benefits that set it apart from traditional savings and investment vehicles. These benefits include:

1. Tax-Deferred Growth

- **How It Works:**
  The cash value in your whole life insurance policy grows tax-deferred. This means you don't pay taxes on the annual growth of your cash value, allowing your wealth to compound uninterrupted.

- **Benefit:**
  By avoiding annual taxes, your money grows faster over time compared to taxable accounts.

2. Tax-Free Loans

- **How It Works:**
  When you borrow against your policy, the loan is not considered taxable income. This allows you to access your cash value without triggering a tax event.

- **Benefit:**
  You can use policy loans to fund major expenses or supplement retirement income without increasing your taxable income.

3. Tax-Free Death Benefit

- **How It Works:**
  The death benefit paid to your beneficiaries is generally tax-free under current U.S. tax law. This ensures that your heirs receive the full value of your policy without tax erosion.

- **Benefit:**
  The tax-free death benefit makes whole life insurance a powerful tool for legacy planning.

4. No Capital Gains Tax

- **How It Works:**
  Unlike traditional investments, the growth in your policy's cash value is not subject to capital gains tax when accessed through policy loans.

- **Benefit:**
  This eliminates a common tax burden faced by investors in stocks, real estate, and other assets.

5. Avoidance of Required Minimum Distributions (RMDs)

- **How It Works:**
  Unlike traditional retirement accounts, whole life insurance policies are not subject to RMDs. You can access your money on your schedule, not the government's.

- **Benefit:**
  This flexibility allows you to manage your retirement income more effectively and avoid unnecessary taxes.

How Infinite Banking Compares to Traditional Tax-Advantaged Accounts

Feature	Whole Life Insurance	401(k)/IRA	Taxable Investment Accounts
Tax-Deferred Growth	Yes	Yes	No
Tax-Free Loans	Yes	No	No
Tax-Free Withdrawals	Yes (via loans)	Only with Roth Accounts	No
Death Benefit Tax-Free	Yes	No	No
Capital Gains Tax	None	Deferred (taxed at withdrawal)	Yes
Required Distributions	None	Yes (after age 73)	No

Tax Strategies with Infinite Banking

To maximize the tax advantages of infinite banking, it's important to integrate your policy into a broader financial strategy. Here's how:

1. Use Policy Loans for Tax-Free Income

- Borrow against your policy to fund retirement expenses or other needs. Because loans are not considered taxable income, this strategy allows you to reduce your taxable income in retirement.

2. Combine with Roth IRAs

- Use a Roth IRA and your whole life policy together to create a tax-free income stream in retirement. Roth IRAs provide tax-free withdrawals, while your policy loans offer additional liquidity without tax consequences.

3. Fund Investments Through Policy Loans

- Instead of withdrawing money from a taxable account and triggering capital gains taxes, use a policy loan to fund investments. This keeps your taxable income lower and allows your cash value to continue growing tax-free.

4. Leverage the Death Benefit for Estate Planning

- Use the tax-free death benefit to cover estate taxes or provide liquidity to your heirs. This ensures your family doesn't have to sell assets to pay taxes or settle debts.

5. Mitigate Taxes During High-Income Years

- During years of high income, borrow from your policy instead of withdrawing from taxable accounts. This reduces your taxable income and potentially lowers your overall tax liability.

The Long-Term Impact of Tax-Free Compounding

To understand the power of infinite banking's tax advantages, consider the impact of uninterrupted, tax-free compounding over time:

Scenario: Tax-Free Growth vs. Taxable Account

- **Taxable Account:**

- Initial investment: $100,000
- Annual growth: 6%
- Tax rate: 25%
  After 30 years, the account grows to approximately $430,000 after taxes.

- **Infinite Banking Policy:**

  - Initial investment: $100,000
  - Annual growth: 6% (tax-free)
    After 30 years, the policy's cash value grows to approximately $574,000, with no tax liability.

This $144,000 difference demonstrates the long-term impact of avoiding taxes on growth.

Common Questions About Taxes and Infinite Banking

1. Are Policy Loans Really Tax-Free?

Yes, as long as the policy remains in force, loans are not considered taxable income. However, if the policy lapses or is surrendered, outstanding loans may become taxable.

2. Does the Death Benefit Always Avoid Taxes?

Under current tax laws, the death benefit is generally tax-free. However, policies that exceed the Modified Endowment Contract (MEC) limit may lose this tax advantage.

3. Can I Deduct Premium Payments?

Premium payments for whole life insurance are not tax-deductible. However, the tax-free growth, loans, and death benefit typically outweigh this disadvantage.

4. What Happens If I Exceed the MEC Limit?

Exceeding the MEC limit converts the policy into a Modified Endowment Contract. While the death benefit remains tax-free, loans and withdrawals may be subject to income taxes and penalties.

Financial Independence Through Tax Efficiency

Infinite banking isn't just about reducing taxes—it's about using tax efficiency to achieve financial independence. By retaining more of your earnings, avoiding unnecessary taxes, and compounding your wealth tax-free, you create a financial system that supports your goals without being eroded by taxation.

Key Steps to Financial Independence

1. Fund your policy consistently to build a strong cash value.

2. Use policy loans strategically to avoid taxable events.

3. Combine infinite banking with other tax-advantaged accounts for a diversified strategy.

4. Recycle money through your policy to maximize growth and minimize taxes.

Conclusion: Leveraging Tax Advantages for a Lifetime

The tax benefits of infinite banking are a powerful tool for building and preserving wealth. By understanding and utilizing these advantages, you can grow your money faster, avoid common tax pitfalls, and create a system that supports your financial independence.

In the next chapter, we'll explore how to sustain and optimize your infinite banking system over time, ensuring it remains a cornerstone of your financial strategy for decades to come. With tax advantages on your side, your journey to financial freedom becomes not just achievable, but inevitable.

Part IV: Overcoming Challenges and Misconceptions

Chapter 10: Common Pitfalls and How to Avoid Them

While infinite banking is a powerful strategy for achieving financial independence and building wealth, its success hinges on proper understanding, execution, and discipline. Missteps can reduce its effectiveness or even jeopardize your financial goals. In this chapter, we'll examine the most common pitfalls people encounter with infinite banking and provide actionable strategies to avoid them.

By the end of this chapter, you'll be equipped with the knowledge to navigate potential challenges, maintain the integrity of your system, and maximize its benefits.

Pitfall #1: Underfunding Your Policy

What It Is:

Underfunding occurs when you contribute less than is necessary to adequately capitalize your policy. This can result in slow cash value growth and limited borrowing power.

Why It Happens:

- Misunderstanding the importance of consistent funding.

- Overestimating short-term financial needs and underestimating the long-term benefits.

- Choosing a policy that doesn't align with your financial capacity.

Consequences:

- Delayed access to cash value.

- Reduced effectiveness of your banking system.

- Missed opportunities for leveraging your policy.

How to Avoid It:

1. **Plan Your Contributions:** Work with your financial advisor to determine a funding schedule that balances your budget with the need to maximize cash value.

2. **Commit to Consistency:** Treat your premium payments as a top financial priority, akin to a mortgage or car payment.

3. **Use Paid-Up Additions (PUAs):** Whenever possible, contribute to PUAs to accelerate cash value growth.

4. **Start Small, Scale Up:** If finances are tight, start with a smaller policy and increase funding over time as your income grows.

Pitfall #2: Overborrowing Without a Plan

What It Is:

Overborrowing occurs when you take out policy loans without a clear repayment strategy, leading to strained cash value and potential policy lapse.

Why It Happens:

- Treating the policy like an unlimited ATM.

- Failing to prioritize loan repayments.
- Borrowing for nonproductive expenses that don't generate returns.

Consequences:

- Reduced cash value growth.
- Increased loan interest costs.
- Risk of the policy lapsing if loan balances exceed the cash value.

How to Avoid It:

1. **Borrow Responsibly:** Only take loans for productive purposes, such as paying off high-interest debt, funding investments, or covering essential expenses.
2. **Set a Repayment Plan:** Treat your policy loans like any other financial obligation by creating a schedule for repayment.
3. **Monitor Loan Balances:** Regularly review your policy statements to ensure loan balances remain manageable.

4. **Avoid Borrowing During the Capitalization Phase:** Wait until your policy has sufficient cash value growth before taking large loans.

Pitfall #3: Choosing the Wrong Insurance Company

What It Is:

Not all insurance companies are created equal, and choosing one that isn't suited for infinite banking can undermine your system.

Why It Happens:

- Lack of research or guidance.

- Selecting a company based on cost alone rather than overall value.

- Working with an advisor who isn't experienced in infinite banking.

Consequences:

- Limited policy flexibility.

- Poor dividend performance.

- Lack of support for infinite banking strategies.

How to Avoid It:

1. **Choose a Mutual Insurance Company:** Mutual companies prioritize policyholders and have a strong history of paying dividends.

2. **Research Financial Stability:** Look for companies with high ratings from agencies like A.M. Best or Moody's.

3. **Work with a Specialist:** Partner with an advisor experienced in designing policies specifically for infinite banking.

Pitfall #4: Focusing Solely on the Death Benefit

What It Is:

Some people mistakenly prioritize the death benefit over cash value growth when setting up their policy.

Why It Happens:

- Misunderstanding the dual purpose of whole life insurance.
- Prioritizing legacy planning over current financial needs.
- Working with an advisor who designs policies traditionally rather than for infinite banking.

Consequences:

- Slow cash value growth.
- Limited borrowing capacity in the early years.
- Reduced effectiveness as a financial tool.

How to Avoid It:

1. **Design for Cash Value Growth:** Work with your advisor to structure the policy for maximum cash value and liquidity, even if it means a lower initial death benefit.

2. **Balance Your Goals:** Consider both your immediate financial needs and long-term legacy planning.

3. **Use Paid-Up Additions:** Contribute to PUAs to boost cash value growth without neglecting the death benefit.

Pitfall #5: Exceeding the MEC Limit

What It Is:

The **Modified Endowment Contract (MEC)** limit is a threshold set by the IRS that determines how much money you can contribute to your policy without losing its tax advantages.

Why It Happens:

- Overfunding the policy too quickly.
- Lack of understanding about MEC rules.
- Poor policy design or guidance.

Consequences:

- Loss of tax-free policy loans.

- Growth within the policy becomes taxable.
- Potential penalties for early withdrawals.

How to Avoid It:

1. **Work with an Experienced Advisor:** Ensure your policy is designed to stay within MEC limits.
2. **Monitor Contributions:** Track your funding to ensure you don't exceed allowable limits.
3. **Adjust Contributions as Needed:** Use flexibility in your policy to balance funding with MEC requirements.

Pitfall #6: Impatience During the Capitalization Phase

What It Is:

The capitalization phase refers to the early years of a policy when cash value growth is slower due to higher insurance costs. Impatience during this phase can lead to abandoning the system.

Why It Happens:

- Unrealistic expectations of immediate returns.
- Lack of understanding about how cash value growth accelerates over time.
- Impatience or financial strain.

Consequences:

- Abandoning the policy before it reaches its full potential.
- Missing out on long-term benefits.
- Lost opportunity for building wealth.

How to Avoid It:

1. **Set Realistic Expectations:** Understand that the benefits of infinite banking compound over time.
2. **Commit to the Long Term:** Treat your policy as a marathon, not a sprint.

3. **Monitor Growth:** Track your cash value growth annually to see incremental progress.

4. **Start Small:** Begin with a policy that fits your current financial capacity to avoid strain during the capitalization phase.

Pitfall #7: Misusing Loans for Nonproductive Expenses

What It Is:

Using policy loans to fund discretionary or nonproductive spending (e.g., vacations, luxury items) without a repayment plan.

Why It Happens:

- Treating policy loans as "free money."
- Lack of financial discipline.
- Failure to prioritize long-term goals.

Consequences:

- Reduced cash value.

- Difficulty repaying loans.
- Erosion of the system's effectiveness.

How to Avoid It:

1. **Prioritize Productive Uses:** Focus on using loans for debt elimination, investments, or income-generating opportunities.
2. **Budget for Repayments:** Plan your finances to accommodate loan repayment.
3. **Treat It Like a Bank Loan:** Approach your policy loans with the same responsibility you would for a loan from a traditional bank.

Pitfall #8: Lack of Regular Review and Optimization

What It Is:

Failing to regularly review and adjust your policy can lead to missed opportunities for growth and system optimization.

Why It Happens:

- Complacency after setting up the policy.
- Lack of understanding about how to maximize its potential.
- Poor communication with your advisor.

Consequences:

- Missed opportunities for additional funding or borrowing.
- Failure to adapt the policy to changing financial circumstances.
- Reduced long-term effectiveness.

How to Avoid It:

1. **Schedule Annual Reviews:** Meet with your advisor regularly to assess policy performance and identify opportunities for optimization.
2. **Stay Informed:** Educate yourself about infinite banking principles and strategies.

Adjust as Needed: Be prepared to modify your contributions, loan strategy, or repayment plans to align with your evolving goals.

Conclusion: Staying on the Path to Success

Infinite banking is a powerful strategy, but like any financial tool, its success depends on how you use it. By understanding and avoiding these common pitfalls, you can ensure that your system remains effective, sustainable, and aligned with your long-term goals.

In the next chapter, we'll explore how infinite banking can be scaled and sustained over multiple generations, ensuring that your personal banking system becomes a legacy of financial independence for your family. With the right approach, infinite banking can become a cornerstone of your financial success.

CHAPTER 11: DEBUNKING THE MYTHS

Infinite banking is a powerful financial strategy, yet it's often misunderstood and misrepresented. Critics and skeptics frequently raise concerns that can discourage individuals from exploring its benefits. However, many of these objections stem from misinformation, lack of understanding, or incomplete analysis. In this chapter, we'll address the most common myths about infinite banking, explain their origins, and provide accurate information to dispel them.

By the end of this chapter, you'll have the clarity to evaluate infinite banking on its merits and confidently respond to any doubts or misconceptions.

Myth #1: "Whole Life Insurance Is a Bad Investment"

The Myth:

Critics argue that whole life insurance offers poor returns compared to traditional investments like stocks, mutual funds, or real estate.

The Reality:

Infinite banking isn't about comparing whole life insurance to investments—it's about creating a financial system that prioritizes stability, liquidity, and control. While whole life insurance may not deliver stock market-like returns, it offers guaranteed growth, tax advantages, and uninterrupted compounding, which are difficult to replicate in traditional investments.

Key Points to Consider:

1. **Guaranteed Growth:** Whole life insurance provides steady, predictable cash value growth, regardless of market conditions.

2. **Uninterrupted Compounding:** Your cash value grows even when you take loans, which isn't possible with traditional investments.

3. **Risk Mitigation:** Whole life insurance shields your money from market volatility, offering a level of security that stocks or mutual funds can't guarantee.

4. **Tax Advantages:** Unlike taxable investment accounts, whole life policies grow tax-deferred and allow tax-free access to funds.

Myth #2: "The Fees Are Too High"

The Myth:

Some critics claim that whole life insurance policies are expensive due to high premiums and administrative costs, making them inefficient for wealth building.

The Reality:

While it's true that whole life insurance premiums are higher than term insurance, the policy serves multiple purposes beyond providing a death benefit. A properly structured policy prioritizes cash value growth and minimizes costs associated with the death benefit.

Key Points to Consider:

1. **Dual Purpose:** Premiums fund both the death benefit and cash value, making whole life insurance a wealth-building tool as well as a protection product.

2. **Paid-Up Additions (PUAs):** Policies designed for infinite banking allocate significant portions of premiums to PUAs, accelerating cash value growth.

3. **Cost vs. Value:** While the upfront costs may seem high, the long-term benefits—tax advantages, compounding, and flexibility—far outweigh the initial expenses.

Myth #3: "It Takes Too Long to Build Cash Value"

The Myth:

Critics often argue that the early years of a whole life policy are inefficient because cash value growth is slow.

The Reality:

The early phase of a whole life policy, known as the **capitalization phase**, is an investment in long-term financial stability. While cash value growth may be slower initially, it accelerates over time due to compounding, dividends, and increasing efficiency.

Key Points to Consider:

1. **Designed for Liquidity:** Policies tailored for infinite banking prioritize faster cash value accumulation, allowing you to access funds sooner.

2. **Long-Term Benefits:** Infinite banking is a marathon, not a sprint. The real power lies in uninterrupted growth over decades.

3. **Patience Pays Off:** By the third to fifth year, cash value growth typically begins to outpace the premiums you've paid.

Myth #4: "I Can Get Better Returns Elsewhere"

The Myth:

Some believe that investing in stocks, real estate, or other assets will provide higher returns than a whole life insurance policy.

The Reality:

Infinite banking isn't about replacing high-return investments—it's about complementing them with a stable, liquid foundation. Your policy acts as a financial buffer, allowing you to invest strategically while mitigating risks.

Key Points to Consider:

1. **Liquidity and Control:** Unlike traditional investments, your cash value is accessible at any time without penalties or market timing risks.

2. **Uninterrupted Growth:** Policy loans enable you to invest while your cash value continues to grow.

3. **Risk Management:** Infinite banking provides a stable foundation that supports other, higher-risk investments.

Myth #5: "Policy Loans Are a Gimmick"

The Myth:

Critics argue that policy loans are just borrowing your own money, and you're still paying interest to the insurance company.

The Reality:

While it's true that policy loans accrue interest, the benefits of borrowing against your policy outweigh the costs. Additionally, the interest you pay goes back into your policy's ecosystem, effectively recapturing the cost of borrowing.

Key Points to Consider:

1. **Uninterrupted Growth:** Your cash value continues to grow as though you never borrowed against it.

2. **Flexibility:** Policy loans don't require credit checks, fixed repayment schedules, or penalties for non-payment.

3. **Recapturing Interest:** By repaying loans with interest, you effectively recycle money into your policy.

Myth #6: "Infinite Banking Is Only for the Wealthy"

The Myth:

Some believe that infinite banking requires substantial income or wealth to implement effectively.

The Reality:

Infinite banking is scalable and can work for individuals at all income levels. The key is starting with a policy that fits your budget and gradually increasing contributions as your financial capacity grows.

Key Points to Consider:

1. **Customizable Policies:** Whole life insurance policies can be designed to fit your financial situation.

2. **Incremental Growth:** You can start small and scale your contributions over time.

3. **Accessibility:** Many people redirect existing savings or debt repayments to fund their policies, making infinite banking more accessible than it seems.

Myth #7: "It's a Scam or Pyramid Scheme"

The Myth:

Some critics mistakenly associate infinite banking with fraudulent schemes due to its unconventional nature.

The Reality:

Infinite banking is based on the principles of whole life insurance, a centuries-old financial product offered by reputable insurance companies. It's a legitimate, legal strategy for managing money more efficiently.

Key Points to Consider:

1. **Reputable Providers:** Infinite banking relies on mutual insurance companies with strong financial ratings.

2. **Transparency:** Policies are fully disclosed, with no hidden fees or unrealistic promises.
3. **Proven Track Record:** Thousands of individuals and families have successfully used infinite banking to build wealth over decades.

Myth #8: "It's Too Complex"

The Myth:

Some people find the concept of infinite banking overwhelming or too complicated to implement.

The Reality:

While the strategy may seem complex initially, a good advisor can simplify the process and guide you step by step. Once your policy is in place, managing it is straightforward.

Key Points to Consider:

1. **Guidance Matters:** Partnering with an experienced advisor ensures your policy is designed and implemented correctly.

2. **Automation:** Premium payments and policy management can be automated, reducing complexity.

3. **Education:** Investing time in understanding the system pays off in long-term financial benefits.

Myth #9: "It's Just a Way to Sell Insurance"

The Myth:

Critics argue that infinite banking is simply a marketing tactic to sell whole life insurance policies.

The Reality:

While whole life insurance is the foundation of infinite banking, the strategy goes far beyond simply owning a policy. It's about creating a personal banking system that aligns with your financial goals.

Key Points to Consider:

1. **Dual Purpose:** Infinite banking uses whole life insurance as a tool for both protection and wealth-building.

2. **Proven Benefits:** The strategy has helped thousands achieve financial independence by leveraging the unique features of whole life insurance.

3. **Long-Term Value:** The emphasis is on building a sustainable financial system, not just selling a product.

Conclusion: Clarity Over Misconceptions

Infinite banking challenges conventional wisdom, which is why it's often misunderstood. By addressing these myths, you can make informed decisions based on facts rather than misconceptions. Infinite banking isn't a one-size-fits-all solution, but for those who commit to understanding and implementing it correctly, it offers unparalleled benefits.

In the next chapter, we'll explore the mindset required for success with infinite banking, emphasizing the discipline, patience, and strategic thinking that drive long-term results. With the myths dispelled, you're one step closer to mastering this transformative financial strategy.

Chapter 12: The Mindset for Success

Infinite banking is more than just a financial strategy—it's a philosophy that requires a mindset shift. To fully reap its benefits, you must adopt new ways of thinking about money, control, and long-term planning. In this chapter, we'll explore the mental habits, attitudes, and disciplines necessary for success with infinite banking.

By the end of this chapter, you'll understand how to cultivate the mindset that drives long-term financial growth, avoids common pitfalls, and ensures the sustainability of your personal banking system.

The Traditional Money Mindset vs. The Infinite Banking Mindset

Traditional Money Mindset

The conventional approach to money often revolves around:

1. **Dependence on Banks:** Trusting financial institutions to manage and grow your money.

2. **Short-Term Focus:** Prioritizing immediate needs or quick returns.

3. **Debt as a Burden:** Viewing debt as inherently negative and something to be avoided at all costs.

4. **Outsourced Financial Control:** Relying on external advisors, employers, or government programs for financial stability.

Infinite Banking Mindset

Infinite banking requires a shift toward:

1. **Financial Independence:** Taking full control of your money and its growth.

2. **Long-Term Vision:** Understanding the power of compounding and uninterrupted growth over decades.

3. **Debt as a Tool:** Viewing policy loans as strategic tools to build wealth.

4. **Personal Responsibility:** Actively managing and leveraging your banking system.

The Core Principles of the Infinite Banking Mindset

To succeed with infinite banking, you must embrace several foundational principles:

1. Patience

Infinite banking is not a get-rich-quick scheme. The benefits compound over time, and the early years often require discipline and commitment.

- **Why Patience Matters:**
    - The first few years involve a capitalization phase where cash value growth is slower.

- o Impatience can lead to abandoning the system before it reaches its full potential.

- **How to Cultivate Patience:**

    - o Set realistic expectations about the timeline for growth.
    - o Focus on incremental progress rather than immediate results.
    - o Regularly review long-term projections to stay motivated.

2. Discipline

Consistency is key to building and maintaining your banking system. This includes funding your policy, repaying loans, and adhering to your financial plan.

- **Why Discipline Matters:**

    - o Irregular contributions or missed loan repayments can disrupt the system's growth.

- o   Discipline ensures that your policy remains a reliable financial tool.

- **How to Cultivate Discipline:**

    - o   Automate premium payments and loan repayments where possible.

    - o   Treat your policy like a real bank: borrow and repay with purpose.

    - o   Develop a monthly or quarterly review habit to track progress.

3. Strategic Thinking

Infinite banking isn't just about owning a policy—it's about using it as a strategic tool for wealth creation.

- **Why Strategic Thinking Matters:**

    - o   Decisions about borrowing, investing, and repaying loans can significantly impact your system's effectiveness.

- Strategic use of funds ensures that you're maximizing returns and minimizing opportunity costs.

- **How to Cultivate Strategic Thinking:**
    - Approach every policy loan with a clear plan for repayment and return on investment.
    - Evaluate how each decision aligns with your long-term financial goals.
    - Work with an experienced advisor to refine your strategies.

4. Ownership

Infinite banking empowers you to take full control of your financial destiny. This requires embracing responsibility and rejecting the traditional reliance on external institutions.

- **Why Ownership Matters:**
    - Success depends on your active involvement in managing and leveraging your policy.

- Ownership fosters a sense of accountability and purpose.

- **How to Cultivate Ownership:**
    - Learn the mechanics of your policy and the principles of infinite banking.
    - Make informed decisions rather than relying solely on advisors.
    - Regularly monitor your policy's performance and growth.

5. Abundance Mentality

Infinite banking operates on the principle that your money can do more than one thing at a time. Shifting to an abundance mentality helps you see the full potential of your system.

- **Why an Abundance Mentality Matters:**
    - It enables you to view money as a tool for growth rather than a finite resource.

- o This mindset encourages reinvestment, expansion, and long-term thinking.

- **How to Cultivate an Abundance Mentality:**
    - o Focus on the opportunities your policy creates, such as financing investments or eliminating debt.
    - o Reinvest the returns from your policy into additional wealth-building strategies.
    - o Celebrate incremental growth as evidence of the system's potential.

Developing Key Habits for Infinite Banking Success

Success with infinite banking isn't just about mindset—it's also about the habits you build. Here are the key practices to incorporate into your routine:

1. Regular Policy Reviews

- **Why It's Important:**

- Tracking your policy's performance ensures you're on target to meet your goals.
- Reviews help you identify opportunities for additional contributions or strategic loans.

- **How to Do It:**
  - Schedule quarterly or annual reviews with your advisor.
  - Monitor cash value growth, loan balances, and paid-up additions.
  - Adjust your strategy as needed to optimize performance.

2. Proactive Financial Planning

- **Why It's Important:**
  - Infinite banking works best when integrated into a broader financial plan.

- o Proactive planning ensures that your policy supports your long-term goals.

- **How to Do It:**

  - o Create a detailed financial plan that includes funding goals, loan usage, and repayment schedules.
  - o Revisit your plan regularly to adapt to changing circumstances.

3. Continuous Learning

- **Why It's Important:**

  - o The more you understand about infinite banking, the more effectively you can use it.
  - o Continuous learning keeps you informed about new strategies and opportunities.

- **How to Do It:**

- Read books, attend seminars, or take courses on infinite banking and personal finance.
- Stay updated on changes in tax laws or financial regulations that may impact your policy.
- Join communities or forums where you can learn from others using infinite banking.

Overcoming Common Mental Barriers

Adopting the infinite banking mindset may require overcoming common mental barriers:

1. Fear of Change

- **The Challenge:** Letting go of traditional financial systems can feel risky.
- **The Solution:** Start small with a policy that fits your current financial capacity. Build confidence as you see results.

2. Scarcity Mentality

- **The Challenge:** Viewing money as finite may make it difficult to invest in a whole life policy.

- **The Solution:** Focus on the long-term benefits of infinite banking and how it multiplies your money's utility.

3. Impatience

- **The Challenge:** The slow initial growth of cash value can feel discouraging.

- **The Solution:** Trust the process and remind yourself of the exponential growth that occurs over time.

The Role of Accountability

Accountability is a crucial component of the infinite banking mindset. To stay on track:

- **Partner with a Trusted Advisor:** An experienced advisor can guide you, answer questions, and provide perspective.

- **Join a Community:** Surround yourself with like-minded individuals who can share insights and experiences.

- **Set Milestones:** Break your long-term goals into smaller, achievable milestones to maintain momentum.

The Mindset for Generational Success

Infinite banking isn't just about your financial future—it's about creating a legacy. Teaching the mindset to your family ensures that the system you build continues to grow across generations.

How to Pass Down the Mindset:

1. **Educate Your Family:** Share the principles of infinite banking and involve them in your financial decisions.

2. **Establish Policies for Future Generations:** Set up whole life policies for your children or grandchildren.

Foster Financial Literacy: Teach younger family members about saving, investing, and leveraging assets responsibly.

Conclusion: Mastering the Infinite Banking Mindset

Success with infinite banking isn't just about having the right policy—it's about cultivating the mindset that allows you to use it effectively. By embracing patience, discipline, strategic thinking, and ownership, you can unlock the full potential of your personal banking system.

In the final chapter, we'll explore how to integrate infinite banking into a comprehensive financial plan, ensuring that it remains a cornerstone of your wealth-building strategy for years to come. With the right mindset, infinite banking isn't just a tool—it's a lifestyle that empowers you to achieve financial freedom and leave a lasting legacy.

PART V: THE BIGGER PICTURE

Chapter 13: The Ripple Effect of Financial Freedom

Infinite banking is more than a financial strategy—it's a catalyst for transforming your life, your family's future, and even your community. By creating a system of perpetual wealth and adopting a mindset of control and independence, you can experience a profound ripple effect that extends beyond your personal finances.

In this chapter, we'll explore the broader implications of financial freedom through infinite banking, from personal empowerment to multi-generational wealth building and community impact. By the end, you'll understand how to maximize the influence of your financial success and use infinite banking as a tool for lasting change.

The Personal Ripple: Empowering Yourself

The journey toward financial freedom begins with you. Infinite banking offers tools and a mindset that empower you to take control of your financial life. Here's how it transforms your personal finances:

1. Freedom from Traditional Financial Systems

- **Breaking Dependency:** Infinite banking reduces your reliance on banks, credit card companies, and other financial institutions. Instead of borrowing on their terms, you set your own.

- **Control Over Your Money:** You decide when and how to access your funds, giving you greater financial flexibility.

2. Confidence and Peace of Mind

- **Financial Security:** Knowing you have a growing, liquid asset to draw from during emergencies or opportunities reduces financial stress.

- **Empowered Decision-Making:** With a strong financial foundation, you can make decisions based on strategy rather than fear or necessity.

3. The Ability to Seize Opportunities

- **Access to Liquidity:** Your policy loans provide immediate access to cash, enabling you to act on time-sensitive opportunities like investments or business ventures.

- **Reduced Risk:** Infinite banking allows you to invest confidently, knowing you have a financial safety net.

The Family Ripple: Building Generational Wealth

One of the greatest strengths of infinite banking is its potential to create generational wealth. By passing on both financial assets and the knowledge to manage them, you can leave a lasting legacy for your family.

1. Teaching Financial Independence

- **Educating Future Generations:** Share the principles of infinite banking with your children and grandchildren to instill financial literacy and responsibility.

- **Involving Them in the Process:** Engage your family in managing the system, teaching them how to fund policies, use loans strategically, and repay responsibly.

2. Funding Policies for Family Members

- **Creating Multi-Policy Systems:** Establish policies for your children or grandchildren to give them a financial head start.

- **A Financial Gift with Long-Term Impact:** Instead of giving cash, fund a whole life insurance policy that grows and provides liquidity throughout their lives.

3. Leveraging the Death Benefit for Legacy Planning

- **Providing Financial Security:** The tax-free death benefit ensures your heirs are cared for financially.

- **Funding Future Policies:** Use the death benefit to establish additional policies for the next generation, perpetuating the system of infinite banking.

4. Reducing Estate Tax Burdens

- **Liquidity for Taxes:** The death benefit can be used to pay estate taxes, ensuring other assets don't need to be liquidated.

- **Efficient Wealth Transfer:** By leveraging the tax advantages of whole life insurance, you can pass on more of your wealth to your heirs.

The Community Ripple: Empowering Others

As your personal and family finances flourish, you're in a position to make a meaningful impact on your community. Financial freedom through infinite banking enables you to contribute to causes you care about, support others in achieving independence, and inspire change.

1. Supporting Local Businesses

- **Using Your Policy for Business Investments:** Provide loans or capital to local entrepreneurs, fostering economic growth in your community.

- **Becoming a Source of Opportunity:** Instead of relying on traditional banks, others can turn to you for fair and flexible financial support.

2. Philanthropy and Giving

- **Funding Charitable Contributions:** Use policy loans to make donations or fund charitable projects without depleting your assets.

- **Creating a Legacy of Giving:** Incorporate philanthropy into your estate planning, using the death benefit to establish scholarships, endowments, or charitable trusts.

3. Sharing Knowledge

- **Educating Others:** Share the principles of infinite banking with friends, colleagues, and community members to help them achieve financial independence.

- **Inspiring Change:** Your success can serve as a model, encouraging others to rethink traditional financial systems and explore alternative strategies.

The Economic Ripple: Changing the Financial Narrative

Infinite banking is a movement that challenges traditional financial systems. As more people adopt this strategy, it has the potential to reshape how wealth is built and preserved on a larger scale.

1. Shifting the Power Dynamic

- **Less Reliance on Banks:** By becoming your own banker, you reduce the power of traditional financial institutions to control your money.

- **More Financial Freedom:** A decentralized approach to wealth management empowers individuals and families to thrive independently.

2. Creating Generational Impact

- **A Stronger Economic Foundation:** Families who practice infinite banking are less likely to experience financial instability, creating a more resilient economy.

- **Increased Capital for Growth:** By recycling money through personal banking systems, more capital is available for productive uses like investments and entrepreneurship.

3. Challenging Conventional Wisdom

- **Questioning the Status Quo:** Infinite banking encourages individuals to think critically about traditional financial advice and explore alternatives.

- **Redefining Wealth Building:** It demonstrates that wealth isn't just about earning and saving—it's about leveraging and recycling money for maximum impact.

Case Studies: The Ripple Effect in Action

Case Study 1: Multi-Generational Wealth Building

- **Scenario:** The Jones family establishes whole life policies for both parents and children. The parents use their policies to fund college tuition and teach their children how to manage the system.

- **Outcome:** By the second generation, the family has multiple policies in place, providing financial security and opportunities for investments. The system continues to grow, benefiting future generations.

Case Study 2: Community Empowerment

- **Scenario:** Maria, a business owner, uses her policy to provide loans to aspiring entrepreneurs in her community.

- **Outcome:** Maria's loans help several small businesses get started. As they succeed, the business owners repay the loans, enabling Maria to reinvest in new ventures. Her community thrives as a result.

Case Study 3: Philanthropic Legacy

- **Scenario:** David uses the death benefit from his whole life policy to establish a scholarship fund for students pursuing careers in healthcare.

- **Outcome:** Over the years, dozens of students receive financial support, fulfilling

David's vision of giving back to his community.

Practical Steps to Maximize the Ripple Effect

1. **Set Clear Goals:** Determine how you want your financial success to impact your family, community, and beyond.

2. **Share the Knowledge:** Teach others about infinite banking and help them implement it in their own lives.

3. **Focus on Sustainability:** Build a system that grows over time and supports multiple generations.

4. **Integrate Giving:** Use your policy to fund philanthropic efforts, whether through donations, loans, or endowments.

5. **Track Your Impact:** Regularly review the results of your efforts, whether it's the growth of your policy, the success of those you've supported, or the legacy you're building.

Conclusion: Transforming Lives Through Infinite Banking

Infinite banking is more than a financial tool—it's a way to create lasting change. By taking control of your money and building a system that supports growth, independence, and generosity, you can positively impact not only your life but also the lives of those around you.

In the final chapter, we'll bring together everything you've learned, providing a step-by-step guide to starting your infinite banking journey and creating a lasting legacy. With the ripple effect in motion, you're not just building wealth—you're shaping the future.

Chapter 14: Infinite Banking and Legacy Planning

Infinite banking is a powerful tool for building personal wealth, but its potential extends far beyond your lifetime. When properly structured and managed, your infinite banking system can create a lasting legacy for future generations. Legacy planning isn't just about passing on wealth; it's about instilling financial principles, empowering your heirs, and ensuring that the system you've built continues to grow and benefit others.

In this final chapter, we'll explore how to integrate infinite banking into your estate and legacy planning, ensuring your financial success has a lasting impact. By the end, you'll have a comprehensive understanding of how to create a system that benefits your family for generations.

What Is Legacy Planning?

Legacy planning is the process of creating a structured approach to passing on your wealth, values, and financial systems to your heirs. With infinite banking, this process takes on an added dimension: you're not just leaving money behind; you're leaving a self-sustaining financial ecosystem.

Goals of Legacy Planning

1. **Wealth Preservation:** Ensure that your assets are protected and efficiently transferred to your heirs.

2. **Wealth Growth:** Create a system that allows your heirs to continue building on your financial foundation.

3. **Financial Education:** Equip your heirs with the knowledge and tools to manage and expand the legacy.

4. **Family Empowerment:** Provide financial security and opportunities for future generations.

The Role of Infinite Banking in Legacy Planning

Infinite banking offers unique advantages that make it an ideal tool for legacy planning:

1. Tax-Free Death Benefit

- The death benefit from your whole life insurance policy is paid to your beneficiaries tax-free, ensuring they receive the full value of your policy.

- This can be used to cover estate taxes, settle debts, or provide immediate financial support to your heirs.

2. Built-In Liquidity

- Unlike other assets, which may require time to liquidate, your policy's death benefit provides immediate liquidity.

- This liquidity can be used to fund other legacy planning strategies, such as creating trusts or funding additional policies.

3. Generational Wealth Building

- Whole life insurance policies can be passed down or used to fund policies for younger generations.

- This creates a perpetual system of wealth that grows over time, benefiting multiple generations.

4. Financial Education Opportunity

- Infinite banking isn't just about leaving money—it's about teaching your heirs how to manage and grow that money.

- By involving your family in the process, you ensure they understand the principles and practices of infinite banking.

Strategies for Legacy Planning with Infinite Banking

1. Establish Policies for Future Generations

One of the simplest ways to incorporate infinite banking into your legacy is by creating policies for your children or grandchildren.

- **How It Works:**
    - Fund whole life insurance policies for younger family members,

setting them up for financial success.

- As they grow, teach them how to use their policies for infinite banking.

- **Benefits:**
  - Provides them with a financial head start.
  - Instills financial discipline and knowledge from a young age.
  - Creates a multi-generational system of wealth building.

2. Use the Death Benefit to Fund Additional Policies

When the death benefit from your policy is paid out, it can be reinvested to expand the infinite banking system.

- **How It Works:**

- o Your beneficiaries use the death benefit to fund new whole life insurance policies.
- o This perpetuates the system, creating additional policies for the next generation.

- **Benefits:**
  - o Ensures that the system continues to grow.
  - o Provides liquidity for new investments or family needs.
  - o Creates a self-sustaining financial ecosystem.

3. Integrate Trusts for Advanced Planning

Trusts can be used in conjunction with infinite banking to provide additional protection and control over your assets.

- **How It Works:**

- o Establish a trust to hold the policy or its proceeds.
- o Define specific terms for how the funds can be used (e.g., education, business investments, or charitable giving).

- **Benefits:**
  - o Protects your assets from creditors or mismanagement.
  - o Ensures your wealth is used in alignment with your values and goals.
  - o Provides tax advantages and reduces the potential for family disputes.

4. Address Estate Taxes with the Death Benefit

For individuals with significant estates, the death benefit can be used to cover estate taxes and other costs, preserving the rest of your assets for your heirs.

- **How It Works:**
  - The tax-free death benefit provides liquidity to pay estate taxes without requiring the sale of other assets.
  - This ensures that your wealth is preserved and passed on intact.
- **Benefits:**
  - Prevents the forced sale of assets like real estate or businesses.
  - Simplifies the estate settlement process.
  - Maximizes the value of your estate for your heirs.

Teaching the Next Generation

A crucial aspect of legacy planning is ensuring your heirs have the knowledge and skills to manage the system you've built. Financial education is key to sustaining and growing the legacy.

1. Share the Principles of Infinite Banking

- Teach your heirs how infinite banking works, including the importance of funding, borrowing, and repaying loans.

- Help them understand the long-term benefits of uninterrupted compounding and disciplined financial management.

2. Involve Them in the Process

- Encourage your children or grandchildren to participate in managing the family's policies.

- Allow them to experience the benefits of using policy loans for investments or major expenses.

3. Provide Ongoing Support

- Act as a mentor, guiding your heirs through the early stages of using their policies.

- Connect them with advisors or resources to ensure they have the tools to succeed.

4. Create a Family Financial Plan

- Develop a comprehensive plan that outlines how the family will use and grow the infinite banking system over time.

- Include specific goals, such as funding education, starting businesses, or supporting charitable causes.

Overcoming Challenges in Legacy Planning

Legacy planning isn't without its challenges. Here are some common obstacles and how to address them:

1. Lack of Financial Literacy

- **Challenge:** Your heirs may not understand the principles of infinite banking or how to manage wealth.

- **Solution:** Invest in financial education, both formal and informal, to ensure they're prepared.

2. Family Disputes

- **Challenge:** Disagreements over how to manage or distribute the legacy can arise.
- **Solution:** Use trusts or written agreements to clearly define roles, responsibilities, and expectations.

3. Policy Mismanagement

- **Challenge:** Poor management of policies can lead to lapses or diminished growth.
- **Solution:** Work with a trusted advisor to ensure policies are properly structured and maintained.

4. Changing Financial Circumstances

- **Challenge:** Economic or personal changes can impact the effectiveness of the system.
- **Solution:** Build flexibility into your plan, allowing for adjustments as needed.

Case Studies: Legacy Planning in Action

Case Study 1: The Multi-Policy System

- **Scenario:** The Smith family establishes whole life policies for parents, children, and grandchildren. Each generation is educated on how to use the policies for infinite banking.

- **Outcome:** Over three generations, the family creates a self-sustaining financial system that funds education, business ventures, and charitable giving.

Case Study 2: Trust Integration

- **Scenario:** John and Mary use their policy's death benefit to fund a trust that provides for their children and grandchildren. The trust specifies that funds must be used for education or investments.

- **Outcome:** The trust ensures the legacy is preserved and used responsibly, benefiting the family for decades.

Case Study 3: Addressing Estate Taxes

- **Scenario:** David has a significant estate, including real estate and investments. His whole life policy's death benefit is used to cover estate taxes, preventing the forced sale of assets.

- **Outcome:** David's heirs inherit the estate intact, along with a growing financial system.

Conclusion: A Legacy of Wealth and Wisdom

Infinite banking offers more than just financial security—it provides a framework for building a lasting legacy. By integrating your policies into a comprehensive legacy plan, you can ensure your wealth benefits future generations while instilling values of financial independence and responsibility.

With careful planning, education, and the principles of infinite banking, you're not just creating wealth—you're creating a system that empowers your family and leaves a lasting impact on the world. As you conclude your journey through this book, you now have the tools, knowledge, and inspiration to take control of your financial future and create a legacy that endures.

Conclusion: Bank on Yourself, Build Your Legacy

You've now taken a deep dive into the concept of infinite banking—a revolutionary approach to managing and growing your money. It's more than just a strategy; it's a shift in how you think about financial independence, control, and legacy. Throughout this book, we've explored the principles, mechanics, and applications of infinite banking, demonstrating how it can transform your financial life and the lives of those around you.

As you close this chapter, let's recap the key takeaways and the steps you can take to embark on your infinite banking journey.

The Key Lessons from This Book

1. Financial Independence Starts with Control

Traditional financial systems often leave you dependent on banks, credit cards, and external lenders. Infinite banking puts the power back in your hands, allowing you to control how your money is saved, accessed, and grown.

2. Whole Life Insurance Is the Foundation

A properly designed whole life insurance policy is the cornerstone of infinite banking. It offers guaranteed growth, tax advantages, and the ability to leverage your cash value for opportunities, emergencies, or investments.

3. The Power of Uninterrupted Compounding

Infinite banking unlocks the magic of uninterrupted compounding. Your money continues to grow even when you borrow against it, creating a financial engine that works for you over the long term.

4. Strategic Thinking and Discipline Are Key

Success with infinite banking requires a mindset shift. Patience, discipline, and a long-term vision are critical for building a system that thrives and supports your goals.

5. Legacy Planning Is the Ultimate Goal

Infinite banking isn't just about personal wealth—it's about creating a self-sustaining system that benefits your family for generations. By teaching financial principles and structuring your system to grow, you leave a legacy of empowerment and security.

Your Next Steps

Now that you understand the potential of infinite banking, here's how to get started:

1. Educate Yourself Further

- Revisit key concepts from this book to deepen your understanding.

- Continue learning through seminars, courses, and conversations with experienced advisors.

2. Partner with an Expert

- Work with a financial advisor or insurance specialist who understands infinite banking.

- Ensure your whole life policy is properly structured to maximize cash value growth and liquidity.

3. Start Small and Scale

- Begin with a policy that fits your current financial situation.
- As your income grows and your understanding deepens, scale your contributions and expand your system.

4. Integrate Infinite Banking Into Your Financial Plan

- Use your policy strategically to address debt, fund investments, and manage major expenses.
- Treat it as the foundation of a broader financial strategy that aligns with your goals.

5. Teach and Share

- Educate your family about the principles of infinite banking.
- Involve them in managing and growing the system, ensuring it becomes a lasting legacy.

A Vision for the Future

Infinite banking is more than a financial tool—it's a philosophy that challenges the status quo and empowers individuals to take control of their financial futures. By implementing this strategy, you're not just building wealth; you're creating freedom, opportunity, and security for yourself and your loved ones.

Imagine a world where you no longer rely on banks or external lenders, where your money works for you at all times, and where your legacy continues to grow for generations. That world is within reach—it begins with the decision to bank on yourself.

Final Words: Take the Leap

As with any worthwhile endeavor, infinite banking requires commitment, patience, and action. The journey may seem daunting at first, but the rewards—financial independence, peace of mind, and the ability to leave a lasting legacy—are more than worth the effort.

Now is the time to take control of your financial future. Start where you are, with what you have, and build the system that will change your life and the lives of those around you.

You've learned the principles. You've seen the potential. The next step is yours.

Bank on yourself. Build your legacy. Live your freedom.

Appendices

Appendix A: Glossary of Key Terms

This glossary provides definitions of key terms used throughout the book to ensure clarity and understanding as you implement infinite banking.

- **Cash Value:** The savings component of a whole life insurance policy that grows over time and can be accessed through loans or withdrawals.

- **Death Benefit:** The tax-free amount paid to the policyholder's beneficiaries upon their death.

- **Dividends:** A share of the profits paid by mutual insurance companies to policyholders, typically used to increase cash value or reduce premiums.

- **Infinite Banking:** A financial strategy that uses whole life insurance as a tool for personal banking, allowing policyholders to save, borrow, and grow wealth on their terms.

- **Modified Endowment Contract (MEC):** A policy that exceeds IRS funding limits, losing some tax advantages. Policies must be structured to avoid MEC status.

- **Paid-Up Additions (PUAs):** Optional contributions to a whole life policy that accelerate cash value growth and increase the death benefit.

- **Policy Loan:** A loan taken against the cash value of a whole life insurance policy, allowing the policyholder to access funds without interrupting cash value growth.

- **Premium:** The regular payment made to maintain a whole life insurance policy, which funds the death benefit and cash value.

- **Uninterrupted Compounding:** The ability of cash value to grow continuously, even when loans are taken against it.

- **Whole Life Insurance:** A type of permanent life insurance that provides lifetime coverage, cash value growth, and a guaranteed death benefit.

Appendix B: Frequently Asked Questions

Q: Can I start infinite banking with limited income?
A: Yes. Policies can be customized to fit your financial capacity, allowing you to start small and scale up as your income grows.

Q: How soon can I take a policy loan?
A: You can typically take a loan once your policy has built sufficient cash value, often within the first year of funding if designed for infinite banking.

Q: What happens if I don't repay a policy loan?
A: Loans don't have mandatory repayment schedules, but unpaid loans will reduce the policy's cash value and death benefit. It's best to have a repayment plan.

Q: Are policy loans taxable?
A: No, policy loans are not considered taxable income as long as the policy remains in force and doesn't lapse.

Q: Can I use infinite banking alongside other financial strategies?
A: Absolutely. Infinite banking complements other strategies, such as retirement accounts, real estate investments, and business ventures.

Appendix C: Resources for Further Learning

Expand your understanding of infinite banking and financial independence with these recommended resources.

Books:

1. *Becoming Your Own Banker* by Nelson Nash
2. *The Bank On Yourself Revolution* by Pamela Yellen
3. *Live Your Life Insurance* by Kim D. Butler

4. *How Privatized Banking Really Works* by Carlos Lara and Robert P. Murphy

Websites and Communities:

- The Nelson Nash Institute: infinitebanking.org

- Bank On Yourself: bankonyourself.com

- Infinite Banking Forums: Engage with like-minded individuals for discussions and advice.

Advisors and Professionals:

- Seek out financial advisors or agents who specialize in infinite banking and have experience structuring policies for this purpose.

Appendix D: Worksheets and Templates

These worksheets and templates are designed to help you organize and manage your infinite banking strategy.

1. Policy Selection Checklist

- Is the insurance company a mutual company? (Yes/No)
- Does the policy allow for Paid-Up Additions (PUAs)? (Yes/No)
- Is the policy designed to avoid MEC status? (Yes/No)
- Have you reviewed the company's financial stability and dividend history? (Yes/No)

2. Funding Plan Template

Year	Base Premium ($)	PUA Contribution ($)	Total Contribution ($)	Projected Cash Value ($)
1				
2				
3				

3. Loan Management Tracker

Loan Purpose	Amount Borrowed ($)	Interest Rate (%)	Repayment Plan ($/mo)	Remaining Balance ($)	Due Date

4. Legacy Planning Worksheet

- Policies to Pass On:
    - Policyholder: _____
    - Beneficiary: _____
- Intended Use of Death Benefit:
    - Pay estate taxes: _____
    - Fund new policies: _____
    - Cover debts: _____
- Family Education Plan:
    - Topics to Teach: _____
    - Resources to Provide: _____

Appendix E: Steps to Get Started

1. **Evaluate Your Financial Goals:**
   Identify your short- and long-term objectives to determine how infinite banking fits into your overall strategy.

2. **Consult an Experienced Advisor:**
   Partner with an advisor specializing in infinite banking to design a policy tailored to your needs.

3. **Choose a Mutual Insurance Company:**
   Select a financially stable company with a strong history of dividend payments.

4. **Structure Your Policy:**
   Ensure the policy is optimized for cash value growth, liquidity, and tax advantages.

5. **Start Funding Your Policy:**
   Begin with a base premium and, if possible, contribute to Paid-Up Additions to accelerate growth.

6. **Plan Your Borrowing Strategy:**
   Use policy loans strategically for debt

elimination, investments, or major expenses.

7. **Review and Adjust Regularly:**
   Monitor your policy's performance and adjust contributions, loans, or repayment plans as needed.

8. **Involve Your Family:**
   Share the principles of infinite banking with your family to ensure the system's longevity and success.

Closing Note

Infinite banking is more than a financial strategy—it's a journey of empowerment, control, and legacy-building. Use these appendices as a guide to support you as you begin implementing the principles of infinite banking and building a life of financial freedom.

www.ingramcontent.com/pod-product-compliance
Lightning Source LLC
Chambersburg PA
CBHW071024240526
45469CB00006BD/2084